Samuel Richardson
& the Dramatic Novel

Samuel Richardson

& the

Dramatic

Novel

IRA KONIGSBERG

University of Kentucky Press

Lexington 1968

Copyright © 1968
University of Kentucky Press

Printed in the United States

Library of Congress Catalog
Card No. 68-29640

To Nancy

Acknowledgments

Parts of the second chapter of this book were first published as "The Dramatic Background of Richardson's Plots and Characters," in *PMLA*, March 1968; and the fourth chapter is a more developed version of "The Tragedy of Clarissa," which was published in *Modern Language Quarterly*, September 1966. I am grateful to the editors of both these publications for permission to reprint the material that first appeared in their journals. A briefer form of Chapter 5 was delivered before The New England College English Association in April 1966.

I wish to express my gratitude to John Loftis of Stanford University, who counseled me during the early stages of this study; to my colleagues at Brandeis University, Benjamin Hoover and Peter Swiggart, who read this work twice and offered much helpful advice; to Ian Watt, who gave sound criticism when it was needed most; to Alan Dugald McKillop, Louis Landa, and Sheridan Baker, all of whom gave assistance on various parts of this work. Most important, I am eternally grateful to my wife, who endured the writing of this book.

Contents

Introduction

Before the novels of Samuel Richardson, English fiction was mostly an inconsequential and undisciplined literary form, written by unskilled writers to entertain the less civilized sensibilities of the reader. The novels of Daniel Defoe were more advanced in technique and less superficial in the presentation of human character, but they still belonged to the tradition of rogue fiction and fell short of Richardson's artistic achievements. The modern novel began with Richardson, and whether or not we are repelled by his puritanism, didacticism, and sentimentality, we must recognize that he did more for the new art form than any other writer of his century. A study of the history of the modern English novel must begin with the pages of *Pamela*, parts I and II (1740-1741), *Clarissa* (1747-1748), and *Sir Charles Grandison* (1753-1754).

By the modern English novel I mean those prose works that create for the reader an illusion of the real world by presenting human personality portrayed in a psychologically realistic manner, involved in probable situations, and dramatically depicted in a physically and temporally conceived universe. As remarkable as they may be, Defoe's novels do not satisfy these requirements. Certainly his major characters are more credible and realistic than those in the fiction of his contemporaries, but his heroes and heroines seem limited because of their overwhelming economic motivation and the brevity or superficiality of their internal reactions, which frequently are not worked into the context of the total work. Also, though the world that Defoe creates may have real objects in it and the characters at moments do seem to move in a universe of space and time, his narrations lack the consistent dramatic dimension that was first to appear in Richardson's novels and was to become one of the basic elements of fiction. Like such seventeenth-century writers of rogue fiction as Francis Kirkman and Richard Head, Defoe attempts primarily to entertain his reader with a large number of exciting adventures experienced by some colorful figure outside the framework of society. The touches of psychological and "circumstantial realism"[1] serve to increase the credibility and intensity of the adventure.

In my estimation Defoe cannot really be called the founder of the modern English novel. *Robinson Crusoe* (1719), *Moll Flanders* (1722), and *Roxana* (1724) must be considered as the furthest development of an earlier form and not the start of another. Defoe never influenced future novelists as Richardson did: Henry Fielding, Fanny Burney, and Jane Austen were part of the tradition established by the author of *Clarissa;* and except for Tobias Smollett, whose works in large part are a throwback to the earlier picaresque tradition, no writer of significance during the eighteenth century even worked the same materials as Defoe.

If Defoe's novels are denied the qualities that make the modern novel modern, the same point applies to almost all the prose fiction of the seventeenth and early eighteenth centuries. Storytelling is one of the concerns of most novels and, indeed, the main function of this earlier literature is to tell stories; but what is expected of the modern novel is picture-making; that is, the ability through words to create in the reader's imagination pictures in depth of people, scenes, and action. The modern novel creates the visual image of a character, with a particular type of mind and personality; it also creates a scene in which people move, talk, and react. Such an ability is mostly absent from earlier fiction, but it dominates Richardson's novels.

Some attempts have been made to explain Richardson's accomplishments in the English novel. Charlotte E. Morgan suggests that early prose fiction significantly influenced his works.[2] But though Richardson adapted the general form of the earlier novel and certain techniques of epistolary fiction, the more significant literary qualities in his novels cannot be accounted for by such literature.

The possible influence of the French novel on Richardson's works has been much discussed; for example, George Sherburn and James R. Foster claim a relationship, while Brian W. Downs and Alan Dugald McKillop deny one.[3] The novelist did not know French, but whether he read any French novels in translation and whether such reading influenced his own fiction are questions that cannot be answered with certainty. Bishop Warburton in a preface to the fourth volume of the first edition of *Clarissa* claimed that Richardson's works had been influenced by a new type of French novel, but in a letter to Warburton the novelist emphatically denied any familiarity with either the French language or writers.[4] Of French fiction printed in English during this period only the novels of Prévost and Marivaux show significant advancements in technique and characterization, and of these the only work that bears resemblance to any of Richardson's novels is Marivaux's *La vie de Marianne*. A translation of the first three parts of *La vie de Marianne* appeared in England in 1736 and probably one of the next four parts in 1737.[5] Yet there is no indication that Richardson ever read these translations. Although he discusses freely in his letters and publications the literature with which he was familiar, his only reference to the French novelist or his works is in the Postscript to *Clarissa* where he quotes a critic who mentions Marivaux as a writer of romance.[6]

For the sake of argument let us suppose that Richardson had read *La vie de Marianne*. Like *Pamela* the French novel is the history of a young girl whose protector tries to make her his mistress.[7] Here resemblance to Richardson's subject matter ends. The characters, plots, and incidents of the two works are utterly different. Though *Marianne* is written in the first person as a memoir, its narrative technique bears only slight similarity to the more dramatic style of Richardson's epistles. Marivaux and Richardson both emphasize sentimental elements in their work, but the French novelist is less insistent in his portrayal of the emotions. It should be remembered that Marivaux was a successful playwright at the time when the French theater was undergoing the same shift in sensibility as the English theater. It is likely that both Richardson and Marivaux were influenced by the artistic trend of their period rather than by each other. *Clarissa* and *Sir Charles Grandison* could hardly have been influenced by Marivaux, since their situations and characters are traceable to other sources, and

3

their literary techniques are clearly developed from those of *Pamela II.*

Ian Watt in *The Rise of the Novel* suggests the whole development of western culture as the cause of the innovations in the eighteenth-century novel. Professor Watt's study is a brilliant treatment of the changes that were taking place in European thought and society, but he fails to relate these changes with sufficient precision to Richardson's artistic innovations. He claims that Richardson's narrative mode reflects "the transition from the objective, social, and public orientation of the classical world to the subjective, individual and private orientation of the life and literature of the last two hundred years."[8] But with the exception of some reference to early epistolary fiction, Watt does not indicate the source of those narrative techniques that underlie Richardson's artistic vision and are in large part responsible for the future development of the modern novel. Also, Watt's claim that Richardson used nontraditional plots is misleading: the novelist's plots were common stock in the contemporary drama. Watt's excellent study of the cultural and social background to Richardson's novels is an insufficient explanation of the rise of the novel because it does not consider the writing of fiction as a craft requiring developed literary concepts and techniques. Watt does not account for the qualities that begin with Richardson and make the novel into an art form.

The theory that I shall present in this work is that Richardson brought to the English novel subject matter and techniques developed in the drama, and that it was the resulting integration of these dramatic elements with fiction which caused the mutation in genre that is responsible for the subsequent course of the English novel. The relationship between Richardson's novels and the drama has only been partially investigated by critics;[9] hence, the full significance of the novelist's indebtedness to the drama in such matters as material, technique, and structure remains unexplored; and, just as important, the ramifications of this indebtedness on the future novel remains unclear. In order to establish those aspects of the drama which influenced Richardson and the general state of fiction at the time that he made his innovations, it is necessary to consider Restoration and eighteenth-century drama and fiction in general as well as Richardson's novels in particular. To be examined also is the development of future fiction in relation to Richardson's innovations.

The objectives of this study impose certain limitations: in order to emphasize and explain fully the effect of the drama on Richardson's novels, I can refer only briefly to other forces that influenced various aspects of his work. The relation of Richardson's novels to preceding epistolary literature has already been established.[10] Earlier epistolary fiction was crude, and I can see little influence of this literature on Richardson except for his general use of the letter form. The concern of this study is not so much with Richardson's use of letters as with the qualities and techniques within each epistle which influenced the future course of the nonepistolary novel. Epistolary fiction itself, with the exception of *Humphry Clinker* and *Evelina,* was not to play a major part in the development of the English novel. The influence of social, religious, and economic ideology has already been discussed adequately by Hill, Watt, and Wendt.[11] Katherine Hornbeak suggests that the novelist's works were influenced by the domestic conduct books of his period.[12] Undoubtedly Richardson's familiarity with such works affected his ideology and resulted in his novels' didacticism and his concern with certain areas of conduct. But Richardson's ideology is not within the scope of this study; his didacticism fits within the framework of his general literary techniques, which were influenced by the drama; and the plots and characters of *Pamela* and the first part of *Clarissa* could hardly have been derived from the codebook's general discussions of the relationship between master and servant and parental responsibility in the selection of a child's spouse.

None of these influences can explain Richardson's remarkable innovations in fiction. The emergence of the modern novel in the eighteenth century is one of the most significant achievements in English letters. What before had been a crude and primitive literary form suddenly was transformed into great art, demanding high seriousness and expert craftsmanship from its writers. The tradition was established to which ultimately would belong the works of Jane Austen, George Eliot, Henry James, and James Joyce. By studying the sources of Richardson's innovations in prose fiction and the ways in which he coalesced elements of one genre with those of another, we can gain a fuller understanding of the development of this new literary form.

CHAPTER ONE

Novelist & Critic
of the Drama

As a boy Richardson chose to be apprentice to a printer because he thought that the position "would gratify" his "Thirst after Reading"; as an apprentice he "stole from the Hours of Rest & Relaxation, . . . Reading Times for Improvement of [his] Mind."[1] That Richardson read much throughout his life is demonstrated by his correspondence and by references in his novels, but his reading, for the most part, was scattered and superficial. Richardson had no knowledge of classical and foreign languages. A statement by Harriet Byron in *Sir Charles Grandison* suggests that the novelist knew the works of the ancients in translation but preferred to read contemporary English authors: "He [Mr. Walden] would needs force into conversation, with a preference to our Shakespeare, his Sophocles, his Euripides, his Terence; of the merits of whose performances, except by translation, no one present but Mr. Reeves and himself could judge" (I, 85).[2] Richardson's puritanical attitude toward literature caused him to distrust the epics of Homer and Virgil: "I am afraid, this poem, noble as it truly is, has done infinite mischief for a series of ages; since to it, and its copy the Eneid [*sic*], is owing, in a great measure, the savage spirit that has actuated, from the earliest ages to this time, the fighting fellows, that . . . have ravaged the earth, and made it a field of blood."[3] He had a general knowledge of the English poets and admired Spenser, Milton, Butler, Cowley, Mason, and Gray; he was also familiar with the essays of Addison, Hill, Cave, Johnson, and Hawkesworth, as well as the works of such theological and philosophical writers as Browne, Taylor, Baxter, Tillotson, and Locke. It is difficult to know just how much prose fiction he had read, for he rarely mentions any specific works of this genre. But Richardson must have read more than a few of his predecessors' novels, since his works do continue several of the general traditions of previous fiction.[4] Nevertheless, he dismissed such literature as too useless and immoral to merit serious attention.[5] On the other hand, Richardson had an intimate knowledge of the English drama, and his writings are filled with comments upon particular plays and the theater in general. His discussions of the drama are not profound and it is obvious that much of his criticism is motivated by bourgeois morality, but it is difficult not to be impressed by his familiarity with the genre.

In 1733, seven years before the publication of *Pamela,* Richardson wrote a short manual of good behavior for young apprentices entitled *The Apprentice's Vade Mecum; Or, Young Man's Pocket Companion.*[6] In the pamphlet Richardson criticizes the immorality of the contemporary drama and warns the young apprentice not to waste his time at the playhouse; such diversions are for people of the "upper life," who can afford to squander their time and money. He attacks the drama for ridiculing sober citizens and tradesmen, but states his admiration for the wit of the comedy of manners. Richardson complains that "genteel comedy" and "noble tragedy" have been replaced by inferior plays, and attacks the pantomimes, dumb-shows, "infamous Harlequin Mimicry," and portrayals of rogues. He eulogizes one drama, however: "I know but one Instance, and that a very late one, where the Stage has condescended to make itself useful to the City-Youth, by a dreadful Example of the Artifices of a lewd Woman, and the Seduction of an unwary young Man; . . . I mean the Play of *George Barnwell* . . . and I could be content to compound with the young City Gentry, that they should go to this Play once a Year, if they would condition, not to desire to go oftener, till another Play of an equally good Moral and Design were acted on the Stage."[7] Lillo's *The London Merchant; or, The History of George Barnwell* (1731) was one of the most significant of the sentimental tragedies, a group of plays that was to have considerable influence on Richardson's fiction. It is likely that the novelist also wrote *A Seasonable Examination of the Pleas and Pretensions of the Proprietors of, and Subscribers to, Play-Houses, Erected in Defiance of the Rogue License* (1735), a short pamphlet that repeats many of the arguments of *The Apprentice's Vade Mecum* and demands that strict regulations be placed on the theater.[8] Richardson never looked upon the drama as a pure art form, existing in its own right and free from society's moral demands. All through his life he considered the theater primarily a means of edification. In this respect he was far from unique in his age.

Richardson's knowledge of drama is also apparent from the discussions of plays that appear in his novels: In *Pamela II* the heroine writes critiques on Ambrose Philips' *The Distrest Mother* (1712), Steele's *The Tender Husband* (1705), and Italian opera;[9] and in *Clarissa* Belford presents one on Rowe's *The Fair Penitent* (1703).[10] Although many of the dramatic quotations in his novels may have come from Edward Bysshe's *The Art of English Poetry*, Richardson's use of such passages at times indicates his familiarity with their sources.[11] For example, the novelist has Lovelace use lines from Shakespeare's *Troilus and Cressida*:

> Thou remembrest what Shakespeare, in his Troilus and Cressida, makes Hector, who, however, is not used to boast, say to Achilles, in an interview between them; and which, applied to this watchful Lady, and to the vexation she has given me, and to the certainty I now think I have of subduing her, will run thus; Supposing the Charmer before me; and I meditating her sweet person from head to foot:
>
> *Henceforth, O watchful Fair-one, guard thee well:*
> *For I'll not kill thee There! nor There! nor There!*
> *But, by the zone that circles Venus' waist,*
> *I'll kill thee; Ev'ry-where, yea; o'er and o'er.*
> *Thou, wisest Belford, pardon me this brag:*
> Her watchfulness *draws folly from my lips;*
>
> .   .   .   .   .

9

Then, I imagine thee interposing to qualify my
impatience, as Ajax did to Achilles:

> *—Do not chafe thee, Cousin:*
> *—And let these threats alone.*
> *Till* accident *or* purpose *bring thee to it.*
>   (IV, 278-79)

Richardson has Lovelace compare the relationship of himself,
Clarissa, and Belford with that of Hector, Achilles, and Ajax.
He further develops Lovelace's characterization by having him
choose these particular lines and present them as he does. At
times Richardson seems to quote merely for decoration, as
when he cites lines from Shakespeare's *Measure for Measure*.[12]
But in general his passages from plays function to suggest
parallels between the novels and the quoted works.

The novelist probably obtained most of his later knowledge
of the theater from reading playbooks and current periodicals.
By the time *Pamela* was published Richardson was plagued by
nervous disorders which might have embarrassed him in public.
He was also quite busy with his two occupations of printer
and novelist and had begun to limit his social life to admiring
flatterers in the confines of his own home. But from his writings
it is obvious that the printer, probably from his earlier years
in London, had a firsthand knowledge of the playhouses themselves and what took place there during a stage performance. In
his *Letters Written on the Most Important Occasions* (1741), a
young country girl, visiting London for the first time, describes
her experiences at the theater.[13] Pamela describes the conduct
of the audience in her letter on *The Distrest Mother:* "The
Pleasure this was receiv'd with by the Men, was equally bar-
barous and insulting; every one turning himself to the Boxes,
Pit, and Galleries, where Ladies were, to see how they look'd"
(IV, 77). Lovelace is familiar with the theater and once discusses the behavior of the contemporary audience: "I have
never given noisy or tumultuous instances of dislike to a New
Play, if I thought it was ever so indifferent: For I concluded,
first, that every one was entitled to see quietly what he paid
for: And, next, as the Theatre (the Epitome of the World)

consisted of Pit, Boxes, and Gallery, . . . those somebodies had as much right to enjoy their own judgements undisturbedly, as I had to enjoy mine" (VII, 91).

Indeed, Richardson considered the theater a significant part of his characters' lives and gave them a knowledge of the drama. Not only does this art form function as a large part of their cultural background but it also serves them as a source of comparisons for their own actions. Throughout *Clarissa* Lovelace envisions himself as a character in a drama: "Sally, a little devil, often reproaches me with the slowness of my proceedings. But in a play, does not the principal entertainment lie in the *first four acts?* Is not all in a manner over when you come to the *fifth?*" (IV, 56) He even thinks of writing a comedy about himself and Clarissa called *The Quarrelsome Lovers* (IV, 50). The extent of this dramatic preoccupation of Richardson's characters is evident from the fact that no sooner does Pamela arrive in London for the first time than she decides to write a book on the drama: "I intend, if it please God to spare my Life, to make a little Book, which I will present to your Ladyship, containing my poor Observations on all the Dramatick Entertainments I have seen, and shall see, this Winter; and for this Purpose I have made brief Notes in the Margin of the printed Plays I have bought, as I saw them, with a Pencil" (IV, 101). Not only does she write the book, but it is read and liked: "I [Lady Davers] thank you for your Book upon the Plays you saw. Inclosed is a List of some others, which I desire you to read, and to oblige me with your Remarks upon them at your Leisure" (IV, 269). Clarissa also has written a book on the drama: "I was at the Play last night with Mr. Lovelace and Miss Horton. It is, you know, a deep and most affecting Tragedy in the reading. You have my Remarks upon it, in the little book you made me write upon the principal acting Plays" (IV, 210). Richardson used his fiction as the basis for other books,[14] and it is probable that he at first thought of issuing a volume of dramatic criticism as written by Pamela, and after the publication of his second novel he considered having Clarissa write one. The following advertisement at the end of Volume IV of *Pamela* suggests as much in relation to the heroine of that novel:

"All the Copies of Mrs. *B.*'s Observation and Writings, upon every Subject hinted at in the preceding Four Volumes, and in particular those relating to *Devotion, Education, Plays,* & c. are now in *One Hand Only:* And that, *if ever* they shall be published, (which at present is a Point undetermined) it must not be, till after a certain Event, as unwished, as deplorable: And *then,* solely, at the Assignment of SAMUEL RICHARDSON" (IV, 457).

It is also significant that Richardson was a printer by trade and that his firm published many plays, most of which he probably read and supervised in publication. Many of the works printed by Richardson have been identified through their ornaments and letterheads,[15] and among these publications are fourteen plays, which include Nathaniel Lee's *Nero* (1674), John Banks' *The Unhappy Favourite* (1681), Susanna Centlivre's *The Gamester* (1705), William Popple's *The Lady's Revenge* (1731) and *The Double Deceit* (1735), Aaron Hill's adaptation of Voltaire's *Alzire* (1736), and Edward Young's *The Brothers* (1753).[16] Undoubtedly Richardson's successful printing firm published more dramas than the fourteen that have been identified.

Also revealing are the novelist's friendships with important men of the theater. One such friend was Colley Cibber. It was probably long after his retirement from the stage, sometime after 1740, that Cibber became acquainted with Richardson. Cibber was then about seventy years of age and, with his bright clothes and foppish airs, was still imitating his former roles in the theater.[17] Richardson by this time had established himself as an expert on morality and had become a teacher of wisdom and virtue to the female world. What could have brought two such seemingly different men together? For one thing, Cibber was an experienced flatterer and must have charmed Richardson's ears with his praise of the novelist's work: "But let me at least do you this agreeable justice, that let your merit, as an author, be whatever it may, yet since I was born I cannot say, that in all my readings of ancient and moderns, I ever met with such variety of entertainment, so much goodness of heart, and so indefatigable a capacity to give proof of it!"[18] Perhaps the novelist also enjoyed the behavior of his friend: Cibber was an occasional visitor to Richardson's home and, with his eccentric mannerisms and rakish actions, probably titillated the novelist and his female friends. But of particular interest to Richardson must have been one aspect of Cibber's theatrical career: as a young man the latter had written *Love's Last Shift* (1696), *The Careless Husband* (1704), and *The Lady's Last Stake* (1707), moral plays that emphasize the virtuous feelings and sentiments of certain characters. In his autobiography the playwright states that in each of his dramas "the Interest, and Honour of Virtue [is] always in view."[19] But it is unlikely that Cibber had a genuine interest in uplifting his audience; he was a practical man and wrote these sentimental comedies to capitalize upon the changing sensibility of the public. Those sentimental qualities which he emphasized more than any playwright before him were developed in the English novel for the first time by Richardson.

Even more enthusiastic about Richardson's works was the author's closest male friend, Aaron Hill. Hill's reputation has not fared well and for good reasons: he was a playwright of little ability, a poet of mean inspiration, and an essayist of mediocre intelligence. But in his own time he was an important figure in the theater and a well-known critic of the contemporary drama.[20] In 1710 Hill was manager and director of Drury Lane and in this position produced three works of his own, including *Elfrid,* which later was rewritten and produced in 1731 as *Athelwold.* In 1721 Hill's *The Fatal Extravagance,* superficially based on *A Yorkshire Tragedy,* was produced under the name of his friend Joseph Mitchell.[21] Ernest Bernbaum calls the play "the first moderately successful domestic tragedy" in the eighteenth century,[22] and Allardyce Nicoll considers it to be the age's first "true bourgeois drama, set in England and without the least attempt at heroicising." According to Nicoll, Hill "deserves the credit, normally given to Lillo, of having been the first to introduce to his age the tragedy of contemporary English types."[23] Hill's relationship with Richardson becomes particularly significant when one realizes that those qualities which distinguish *The Fatal Extravagance* also make *Clarissa* the first domestic and sentimental tragedy in novel form in the history of English literature. As well as writing other dramas, Hill also translated Voltaire's *Zaïre, Alzire,* and *Mérope*: the first two translations were produced in 1736 and the third in 1749.

From 1734 to 1736 Hill edited and wrote most of the essays for *The Prompter,* a periodical devoted mainly to theatrical news and criticism. Richardson's printing firm published *The Prompter,* and the novelist seems to have assisted Hill in his management of the periodical.[24] But their friendship seems to have begun some years before.[25] In 1736 Richardson's firm also published Hill's *Alzira.* Richardson sent Hill a copy of *Pamela* in 1740 and Hill's subsequent letters are filled with expressions of admiration for the novelist's work. In 1746 Richardson published the first part of *The Art of Acting,* Hill's verse account of his theory of acting, an earlier version of which had appeared in *The Prompter.* Thomas Davies in his *Memoirs of the Life of David Garrick* (1780) said of Hill that he was "almost the only gentleman [of his time] who laboured assiduously to understand the art of acting, and who took incessant pains to communicate his knowledge of it to others."[26]

Hill and Richardson exchanged a great many letters during a fifteen-year period. Indeed, Hill seems to have been the novelist's closest friend, and it is evident that both men had much in common—both enjoyed discussing Richardson's works, both were prolific letterwriters, and both were deeply concerned with the contemporary theater.

Richardson also knew Edward Young, author of *Night Thoughts* (1742–1745) and *Conjectures on Original Composition in a Letter to the Author of "Sir Charles Grandison"* (1759). Of interest are the one hundred and fifty letters exchanged by the two authors and published in the *Monthly Magazine* from 1813 to 1819.[27] In these letters Richardson's influence on the development of Young's *Conjectures* can be traced. But Young was also a playwright. *Busiris, King of Egypt,* an unimpressive, violent tragedy, was produced in 1719. *The Revenge,* based on Shakespeare's *Othello* and produced in 1721, is a better play and was received kindly by the public. *The Brothers* appeared in 1753 and, according to Richardson, did not have much success.[28] Richardson's firm printed *The Revenge* in 1753.

Another close link between Richardson and the theater may be seen in the novelist's relationship with David Garrick. In his Postscript to the first edition of *Clarissa,* Richardson had suggested that the time was right for a production of the original *King Lear,* for "an *Actor* and a *Manager,* in the *same person,* is in being, who deservedly engages the public favour in all he undertakes" (VII, 428).[29] Richardson sent Garrick three volumes of *Clarissa* and soon received a letter in which the actor thanked him for the gift and regretted that they had not met for so long.[30] In 1748 Hill wrote to Richardson and expressed his fear that Garrick purposely was delaying the production of his *Meropé* in order to produce Johnson's *Irene* and Thomson's *Coriolanus.*[31] Richardson's response defends the actor and supplies interesting information about the theater of that period: "As to Mr. Garrick, give me Leave to say what I know: which is: That he was actually long ago engaged in Irene. The Author was his Tutor; and it was expected to come on last Season. Mr. Garrick had also engaged to Mr. Lyttelton, that no new Play should be acted during the Run of Coriolanus."[32] The relationship between Garrick and Richardson seems to have begun about the time that *Clarissa* was first published and to have lasted until the novelist's death.

Also of interest is Richardson's association with the playwright Edward Moore. Moore wrote *The Foundling* (1748) and *The Gamester* (1753), two dramas of some distinction with sentimental qualities similar to those in Richardson's works. The novelist seems to have been introduced to the playwright by Garrick. Moore began a dramatic adaptation of *Clarissa* but never completed the play.[33] A letter to Richardson from Mrs. Delaney, dated 24 April 1747, suggests a possible reason why the work was not completed: "I am glad Mr. Moore did not go on with his design of making a tragedy of Clarissa; the alteration he proposed in making the heroine more in love would have taken off the delicacy and polish of her character."[34] Richardson may have objected to the dramatist's plans for Clarissa and put an end to the project. But the novelist knew and appreciated

Moore's works, and said of *The Gamester,* "I heard the greatest part of the *Gamester,* read by Mr. Garrick, before it was brought upon the stage. On the whole, I much like it. I thought it a very affecting performance. There are faults in it; but I think it a moral and seasonable piece."[35]

Perhaps Richardson's friendship with these men is the most interesting aspect of his relationship to the drama. The total careers of Cibber, Hill, and Garrick span almost a century of English theater. Cibber and Hill were managers of the Drury Lane theater and both were prolific playwrights. They professed the same enthusiasm as Richardson for the moral improvement of the stage and, along with Moore, wrote important plays which emphasized a new sensibility that influenced Richardson's novels. It now seems obvious that Richardson had a strong interest in the English drama and an excellent knowledge of the genre. What remains to be established are the ways in which this interest and knowledge affected his novels.

CHAPTER TWO

Maidens & Libertines

In *Pamela* are a rich gentleman and a beautiful, virtuous, but impoverished maiden; these characters are attracted to each other and after overcoming certain obstacles are united. This is a version of what might best be called the Cinderella myth.[1] For that matter, Griselda and Walter, Jane Eyre and Rochester, and Sally and Matt Monday also are Cinderellas and Prince Charmings. Life is comprised of those who have and those who have not, and from time immemorial the less fortunate have desired to become the more fortunate. The natural way for a person in the lower class to achieve a better life has always been through marriage; the unnatural way through revolution. The universal tale of the daughter of the poor who has certain sacred virtues and marries a member of the wealthy class is a result of such desires. The tale pleases the lower class by giving hope for social advancement, and satisfies the higher class by fostering equilibrium in society and giving expression to its males' desire to possess women more earthy than women of their own class.

But each society gives to the myth a different emphasis and new details; for example, although the stories of Griselda and Walter and of Pamela and Mr. B. have much in common, they are quite different in their basic moral codes, social worlds, and in the personalities of their characters. My interest is in the Cinderella myth as it appeared during the Restoration and early eighteenth century. This period, because of the nature of its social classes and their respective moralities, was receptive to this type of story, and when Richardson wrote *Pamela* he was one of many authors who had clothed the myth in the garments of his age. The novel's basic story-pattern is universal, but its moral focus, social reality, and characterizations relate it to other works that appeared in contemporary literature.

McKillop believes that the content of *Pamela,* rather than being influenced by any specific literature, "fall[s] in with a general literary drift" of the age.[2] The works that he discusses are useful in my context, for they show how little Richardson could have obtained even from the nondramatic literature that most resembles *Pamela.* The literature first mentioned by McKillop has in common with Richardson's novel only the subject of a wealthy gentleman's love for a poor girl; none of these works has the same plot or character types as *Pamela.* Closer to Richardson's work is the story told by John Hughes in *Spectator* No. 375: "The sketch has in common with *Pamela* the formal offer of 'keeping' from the licentious lord to the heroine and the righteous indignation, conveyed by letter, of her distressed parents." But McKillop points out the works are dissimilar in that "the heroine [of the sketch] is not of lowly origin, and virtue, without undergoing a long siege, is quickly rewarded." It is even more significant that the story is told in only a few paragraphs, and there are no developed characters and scenes. Another parallel that McKillop mentions is the brief summary of a story related in Captain Alexander Smith's *School of Venus* or *Court of Venus* (1716); but here there are many dissimilarities—for example, the girl is "abducted, seduced, and cast upon the town"—and again there are no developed characters and scenes. Unquestionably these works are as close as we can come to *Pamela* in nondramatic literature, but they lack both the plot development and the basic character types of Richardson's novels.

One particular variation of this Cinderella story did appear in the drama, however, with character types and actions different from and more developed than those in versions of the myth to be found in other literary forms. Richardson's *Pamela* possesses these same elements and even similar passages to such an extent that it is impossible, I believe, not to associate it with such plays.

Themes of seduction and attempted seduction were quite popular in the drama of the Restoration and early eighteenth century, more so than in the literature of any other period in English history. The sexual themes of the Restoration comedies of manners were in part a reaction to the Commonwealth suppression of animal spirits; and the sexual themes of the moral dramas that appeared during the last part of the seventeenth and early decades of the eighteenth centuries were in part a reaction to the Restoration comedies. Both *Pamela* and *Clarissa* are related to this latter group of plays, which attacked sexual lust and eulogized virtue.[3] Such plays reflect the developing middle-class concern with the morality of the theater but they also suggest the prurient fascination of the audience with these works' characters and subject matter. The history of the sexual mentality of the English during these centuries was one of shifts, unbalance, and frustration—a pietistic Commonwealth yielded to an exuberant Restoration, which in turn gave way to a period of self-consciousness. In conflict during the last period were public impulses of license and censure, and when the playwrights censured to satisfy the moral sense in their public and in themselves they also had to satisfy the sexual passions. The result was that these "reforming" dramas took on certain characteristics and a general ambivalence in tone. Richardson, who was also concerned about the immorality of the stage, employed in *Pamela* and the second part of *Clarissa* character types and situations used by playwrights to advocate "virtue"; and his treatment of such material suggests the same sexually ambivalent attitude as that of the dramatists.[4]

The central plot of Richardson's *Pamela* was foreshadowed as early as 1647 by the subplot of Thomas Brewer's *The Countrie Girle*. A plagiarized version of the play by John Leanerd, *The Country Innocence; or, The Chamber-Maid Turn'd Quaker*, was produced in 1677. I shall cite the latter work because it is closer to Richardson's own time, and there is more chance that the novelist was familiar with it. The major part of *The*

Country Innocence is concerned with a reluctant widow and her eager suitors. The secondary plot is concerned with a tenant's daughter named Margaret, who fights the advances of Sir Robert Malory, the lord of the manor. Sir Robert, in his attempts to seduce the girl, has conversations with her that are typical of many in *Pamela*:

> *Mar.* Why, Sir, the Education, that fair Breeding you have bestow'd upon my Poverty has made me what I am, and plentifully furnished my Soul with all that best adorns her, that whatever is in opposition to it, is—
> *Sir Rob.* What?
> *Marg.* Your Lust, Sir *Robert*: I am bold, but yet can kneel to beg your mercy for it. [Kneels.]
> *Sir Rob.* What? [*sic*] she imagines Water to my Flame, is Oyl t'increase it. The more she puts it off, the more she pulls me to her. Come, come rise, though you be so unkind, I can forgive you.⁵   (II, i)

This is reminiscent not only of Richardson's two leading characters and their scenes of confrontation but also of the novelist's moral, sentimental, and sexual preoccupations. Unlike Mr. B. in *Pamela*, Sir Robert does not offer wealth as a bribe to the maiden; rather it is his wife who makes the offer when pretending to be a bawd for her husband. When Margaret angrily refuses the bribe, Lady Malory is convinced of the girl's virtue and joins with Margaret and her family to cure Sir Robert of his lust. Margaret is a well-educated and mature woman, capable of being a fit companion to her master, who, however, is married; but her virtue is rewarded through the attainment of money, the promise of a good husband, and the improvement of her family's position. Thus, the basic elements of *Pamela* appear in *The Country Innocence*—such characters as the sexually frustrated libertine master, the passionately virtuous country maiden, and the girl's humble father; the scenes of virtue in distress but always triumphant; the frequent platitudes concerning chastity; and the excessive emotionalism of Richardson's novel are all present in this Restoration play. But a social atmosphere in which the two leading characters could be married is lacking; hence, virtue cannot raise the chaste maid to the highest honors as it will do in later dramas and in Richardson's novel.

Another play with similarities to *Pamela* is *The Country Lasses; or, The Custom of the Manor* (1715) by the popular eighteenth-century playwright Charles Johnson, whose *Caelia* (1732) probably influenced Richardson's *Clarissa. The Country Lasses* was produced throughout the first half of the eighteenth century: in the decade before the publication of *Pamela* it received numerous performances, and in 1740, the year of the novel's appearance, it was performed five times.[6] The major plot of the drama is concerned with the romances of Modely and Heartwell. Tired of the routine pleasures of the city, these young gentlemen come to the country for diversion, and each immediately begins the long, arduous task of trying to seduce an impeccable country maiden. The relationship between Heartwell and Flora is similar to that between Pamela and Mr. B.: the libertine attempts to buy the girl's innocence, but she replies by eulogizing her virtue and her humble birth:

> *Heart.* . . . I will settle 200*l.* a year upon you for Life, and provide for all our Children.
>
> .   .   .   .   .
>
> *Flora.* . . . all the Inheritance I boast or wish for, is this low humble Cottage, and a Mind, I hope a virtuous Mind, that cannot even in this Situation bear Dishonour.
>
> .   .   .   .   .
>
> *Flora.* . . . My Father, whose prop I am, the stay of his old Age; taught me with pious Care to tread the Paths of Virtue; how wou'd it tear the Strings of his old Heart to see me faln at once to Shame and Infamy? . . .
> *Heart.* Oh, thou hast touch'd my Soul! I *feel* thy Words; a conscious Pang stabs thro' my Heart, and covers me with Shame.   (IV, i)

These lines are similar to many in *Pamela,* whose heroine is also fond of discussing her virtue in relation to her father and poverty: "Yes, Sir [Mr. B.], as *poor* and as *honest* too [her father], and that is my Pride. Says he, I will do something for him, if it be not your Fault, and make all your Family happy. Ah! Sir, said I, he is happier already than ever he can be, if his Daughter's Innocence is to be the Price of your Favour. And I beg you will not speak to me on the *only* Side that can wound me" (I, 108). But Flora, more easily than Pamela, is able to convert her would-be seducer and marry him. The conflict between Modely and Aura is similar to that between Heartwell and Flora, except that Modely is less willing than Heartwell to be converted. Modely attempts to seduce Aura, but is caught by her father, Freehold, and severely lectured not only as an individual but also as a member of a corrupt social class. Free-hold denounces Modely in terms that suggest Richardson's bourgeois attitude toward the upper class in *Pamela* and *Clarissa*.[7] Modely is finally converted at the end of the play. Heartwell discovers that Flora is Lady Betty and that he is thus lord of the manor. The play concludes with Heartwell's stating, "there is no real lasting Good but in Virtue."

Heartwell and Modely are similar to Mr. B. in many aspects of their personalities and in their general actions. Heartwell at first is like the libertine Mr. B., who attempts to seduce the country maid; later, when he is made aware of his cruel behavior, he reforms. Realizing the merits of the girl's virtue, he desires to marry her in spite of the apparent inequality between their social positions.[8] He thus foreshadows the newly converted Mr. B., though he is more sentimental and susceptible to reformation. Modely, a full portrayal of the English rake, desires to possess women, regardless of the inconveniences it might cause his victims. It is only at the end of the play, after he has been sufficiently ridiculed and abused, that he is willing to marry Aura, a girl far below him in social position. Modely, then, for most of the work, is the same character type as Mr. B. before his conversion—unfeeling, selfish, lustful, intriguing, and seemingly concerned with only one objective in life. On the other hand, Aura is certainly no Pamela, for she is too flirtatious, clever, and sophisticated. Flora is also sophisticated, but she is more like Richardson's heroine: she is obsessed with virtue and anticipates Pamela's morality, sentimental qualities, sexual consciousness, and pride in poverty. But she always is decorous and shows a worldly wisdom and maturity that Pamela never possesses. Freehold bears little similarity to his counterpart in Richardson's novel. He is a poor farmer who formerly was wealthy, but there his similarity to old Mr. Andrews ends. Pamela's father, once a prosperous middle-class businessman, is now humble, tearful, and sentimental. Freehold formerly was a city playboy, but the loss of his fortune and a series of disappointments have driven him into retirement. He is now proud, independent, and cynical.

The Country Lasses, then, presents two relationships similar to that between Margaret and Sir Robert in *The Country Innocence* and to that between Pamela and Mr. B. in Richardson's novel. Charles Johnson portrays the conflicts between virtuous maidens and well-born libertines as struggles between sexual chastity and male aggressiveness; one of these relationships is characterized by pathetic emotions and moral platitudes. Unlike Leanerd, Johnson suggests that virtue equalizes all ranks by having the well-born Heartwell marry the seemingly poor Flora and by indicating that Modely eventually will marry a maiden of the lower class on account of her virtue. Like *Pamela,* the play is filled with sentiments attacking the licentiousness of the upper class and praising the virtues of the humbly born.

George Lillo, one of the leading playwrights of the first half of the eighteenth century and an author of whom Richardson was well aware, also presented this type of story in a ballad-opera called *Silvia; or, The Country Burial* (1730).[9] It was Lillo's first produced play and contained much of the excessive sentimentality that was to be an essential element in his later works. *Silvia* is about a rich nobleman who falls in love with a poor girl and attempts to seduce her. He offers her wealth, but the maiden gives him the usual answer about her humble birth and virtue: "Know, thou ungenerous Man, I ne'er was influenced by thy Wealth to hearken to thy Vows; for notwithstanding my humble Birth, and Fortune, I ever scorn'd Riches, when compar'd to Love, as now I do Love and Thee, compar'd to Virtue" (I, iv).

The following speech by Pamela suggests the similar themes and basic situations of the play and the novel, as well as their very similar heroines: "Here, said I, were my poor honest Parents; they took care to instil good Principles into my Mind, till I was almost Twelve Years of Age; and taught me to prefer Goodness and Poverty to the highest Condition of Life" (I, 273). Like Mr. B., Sir John finally decides to marry the virgin in spite of her low birth. There is little discussion of social inequality by the lovers. Welford, Silvia's supposed father, also seems unimpressed by the rank of the girl's suitor and rejects Sir John because of his immorality. The lovers eventually marry despite the discovery of Silvia's noble birth and Sir John's mean origins. Lillo thus permits a greater breach of social law than Richardson was to allow by the union of Mr. B. and Pamela. Although a man could never lose social status through marriage, a woman could elevate or lower her position according to the rank of her husband. Pamela's status was elevated by her marriage; that of Silvia was considerably lowered.

Lillo, in one respect, was more careful than Richardson in the portrayal of his heroine. Henry Fielding and other contemporaries of Richardson accused Pamela of being something of a fortune-hunter, willing to barter herself for an advantageous marriage.[10] After all, Mr. B. had behaved outrageously toward her, but was accepted as a husband the moment he proposed. Pamela, they claimed, was motivated throughout her ordeal not so much by virtue as by a sound business sense. Richardson, of course, had not intended her action to be interpreted in such a way, but in his enthusiasm to have virtue rewarded he allowed Pamela to accept the marriage offer too hastily. Lillo, on the other hand, had Silvia refuse Sir John in the belief that in marrying the man who had so offended her, she would make her previous virtue seem a ruse to obtain a better offer. A marriage between the victim and her oppressor created a moral problem that Lillo was quick to realize; Richardson failed to see the problem because of his preoccupation with the themes of sexual chastity and virtue's rewards. But Lillo's solution of switching the protagonists' births in order to remove any financial rewards for his heroine in marrying her would-be seducer is neither morally nor dramatically satisfying.

Lillo's play possesses certain elements that had not appeared earlier in the drama and that were later to be part of Richardson's novel. The servants in Sir John's household have a more prominent part than those in the plays discussed previously. The wicked Jonathan, for example, though not at all like the goodhearted butler of the same name in *Pamela,* is similar in function to Mr. B.'s servants John Arnold and Colbrand. Lettice and her parents in the play are presented as contrasts to Silvia and Welford: Lettice's loss of virtue and the shame she and her parents experience help bring into prominence the virtue and pride of Silvia and Welford. Richardson also uses the shame of a fallen woman to heighten his heroine's virtue and its rewards when Mr. B. relates to Pamela his affair with Sally Godfrey. Thus, not only do we find in this play a similar plot and the same types of hero and heroine as those in *Pamela,* but the drama and novel even contain similar minor actions and characters.

Silvia was popular enough to be parodied by Henry Fielding in the subplot of *The Grub-Street Opera,* published in 1731.[11] Silvia and Sir Robert are satirized in the play by Molly and Owen in much the same manner that Pamela and Mr. B. were to be represented by Shamela and Squire Booby ten years later in Fielding's *Shamela.* The story of the virtuous country maiden who, for the sake of her chastity, spurns the advances and promises of her noble but decadent master is brilliantly ridiculed in *The Grub-Street Opera.* Molly's virtuous speeches are fanatically passionate and comical: "Avaunt—a blight is in thy kiss—thy breath is the wind of wantonness—and virtue cannot grow near thee" (II, ii).[12] Owen's portrait is harshly satirical. But the girl's father, Mr. Apshones, is not a comic figure: he is honorable, proud, and outspoken, often uttering what seem to be Fielding's own sentiments.

The relationship between Owen and Molly also satirizes the attitude toward sex which is apparent in many other dramas of the period, as does the major plot, which depicts the romance between the servants Robin and Sweetisa.[13] In *The Grub-Street*

Opera Fielding's female characters are a satirical commentary on the theater's frequently unrealistic, ridiculous, and often hypocritical preoccupation with chastity. In his *Shamela* and *Joseph Andrews,* Fielding was later to ridicule the same moral attitudes of *Pamela.* The very fact that Fielding satirizes in his play these attitudes and the character types of the pursuing rake and the innocent maiden manifests their significance in the drama nine years before the publication of *Pamela.*

In a letter to the Reverend Johannes Stinstra, the novelist declared that the story of *Pamela* had been suggested to him fifteen years before its composition by a friend's narration of a true-life adventure.[14] Dottin and McKillop believe that though the germ of the story may have had its origin in this source, it is hardly possible that the novelist would have remembered details related fifteen years earlier. They think that the particulars of the story in the letter to Hill were suggested to Richardson by *Pamela* itself.[15] Richardson's comments on the source of *Pamela* indicate only that he may not have derived the basic theme of the work from the drama and that he may not have imitated any single play. But so much in the novel is similar to what had appeared in the theater that the relationship can hardly be one of chance. Richardson received the impetus to write *Pamela* from his initial exploration of the story in epistles CXXXVIII and CXXXIX of *Letters Written on the Most Important Occasions;* but he derived much of his material and many of his ideas for the treatment of his theme from the art form with which he was most familiar, the Restoration and early eighteenth-century drama.

By the time Richardson began to write his novel, the character types and basic story of *Pamela* had been developed in the theater. Already in existence was a type of heroine similar to Pamela. The extremely virtuous maiden of the drama was poor, beautiful, and proud. She had a fine intelligence and possessed a considerable awareness of sex and society; in spite of her modesty, she was outspoken in matters of virtue and chastity. Margaret, Flora, and Silvia are all sophisticated, mature women. Flora is of noble birth, but both Margaret and Silvia have been raised by poor parents in rural settings. Nevertheless, a humble background is not evident in any of these characters. Their sophistication is emphasized by the awkward countryfolk around them. None of these heroines is particularly real or complex; they are all concerned primarily with keeping their chastity and exhibiting their morality. Richardson may not have made his heroine more believable, but he removed any unnatural sophistication from her. In his novel the maiden became a very young, generally crude, and excessively pathetic creature. Richardson expanded into a full-length novel what before had been presented in the short duration of a play; by devoting so many pages to the sexual temptations that beset one girl, and by having her constantly discuss her own virginity, he made his heroine a distorted and frequently boring creature. Possessing too much sentimentality and outspokenness while lacking the intelligence and maturity of Flora and Silvia, Pamela is neither attractive nor sympathetic. Richardson was so concerned to have his heroine's virtue rewarded that he failed to see that her marriage to a man who had maliciously attacked her chastity might make her appear calculating and ambitious. It is only in those peripheral scenes when Pamela is not fighting or lecturing Mr. B. that she attains a sympathetic girlish quality.

By 1740 the basic characterization of Richardson's rake also had been developed in the drama. The libertine was well-born, wealthy, and selfish, but he possessed sensibility sufficient for his moral conversion at the end of the play. Sir Robert, Heartwell, and Sir John are all obsessed with lust and willing to relinquish handsome portions of their wealth to have their desires fulfilled, but each finally is made aware of the maiden's moral superiority and his own evil ways. Heartwell and Sir John discover that their sexual desires have turned to love. All the libertines are so possessed by lust during the first part of the work and are so excessive and unnatural in their repentance during the remainder of the play that they display few aspects of human personality. Nor is Richardson's Mr. B. any more developed or credible. At the beginning of the novel, when he is passionate and scheming, his sexual hunger for a mere servant girl is crudely portrayed. After his conversion, based on no earlier evidence of moral sensibility, and even more sudden than the repentance of the rakes in the drama, he emerges as a completely different character. The new Mr. B. is a distorted and unconvincing version of the country gentleman, and little more than an obnoxious prig.

Richardson's Goodman Andrews only slightly resembles the maidens' fathers in the drama. His function in the novel is the same, but his characterization differs. In *The Country Innocence* Thrashard is a nonentity who must be forced to see his master's evil ways. In *The Country Lasses* Freehold is a retired malcontent who suspects everything about the upper class. Welford in *Silvia* bears closer resemblance to Andrews, but he is stronger and far less pathetic. Goodman Andrews fulfills the role of a father concerned with the well-being of his child and the maintenance of his family's honor, but in an excessively sentimental manner. He is portrayed condescendingly as a very poor, ignorant, humble, virtuous, and suffering countryman.

Richardson also retained the general plot of the dramas, though extending its duration and adding such characters as Mrs. Jewkes, Mrs. Jervis, Parson Adams, and Lady Davers for needed complications. He also added to the plot a considerable amount of intrigue and sexual machination and an occasional building of suspense. But Richardson added little that was strikingly new to the material that had appeared in the drama. It is not the general plot of *Pamela,* however, that holds our interest, nor is it just the fact that the novel is a version of the Cinderella myth. It is rather the occasional sweep of the narrative, the vivid and dramatic presentation of certain scenes, the frequent fervor of sex, and the unusual and sometimes distorted presentation of certain characters which make the work interesting to the modern reader.

Clarissa is composed of two related parts, the first dealing with the heroine's enforced betrothal, and the second with her rape.[16]

The former is a contemporary version of the universal theme of the rebellious child struggling with despotic parents in order to achieve independence. In a society in which matrimony is an important means of alliance between families, the theme of the conflict between generations often appears in literature as the story of enforced betrothal. In the Restoration and eighteenth century the family generally was motivated by economic considerations in its view of marriage.[17] Such motives were considered moral in such a mercantile society, and a child who acted against the welfare of the family was viewed as immoral. But if parental approval was necessary for marriage, it was commonly accepted that a child did have the right, ultimately, to refuse an undesired alliance. Many families, however, did not want to grant such a privilege to children. Parental wills clashed with children's demands in the matter of marriage, and one of the results was the recurring literary story of an enforced betrothal of a virtuous daughter, which was treated in such a way as to emphasize the conflict between family and private duties.

The problem of enforced betrothal was sometimes discussed in such conduct books as Defoe's *The Family Instructor* (1715), but not presented there in a novelistic manner. Sketches based upon the theme occasionally appeared in the periodical essay, but they do not at all resemble Richardson's developed treatment of the subject. For example, in *Spectator* No. 164, written by Addison, two romantic lovers, Constantia and Theodosius, separate and ultimately join religious orders because of the heroine's enforced betrothal; and in *Spectator* No. 220, written by Steele, an outraged woman writes a rather ill-mannered letter to the elderly man whom her father wishes her to marry. Writers of fiction also treated the subject quite differently from Richardson. In *Luck at Last; or, The Happy Fortunate* (1723) by Arthur Blackmore[18] Sosander orders his daughter Sylvia to marry Stertorius, but the suitor is quite elderly and his relationship with the girl resembles the typical January-May relationship of literature, except that Sylvia is virtuous and, rather than marry the old man, runs off and becomes a servant. Mrs. Haywood in *The Fatal Secret; or, Constancy in Distress* (1724) also describes an enforced betrothal, but here the young woman, who is presented much like the heroines of the French Romance, feels a violent passion for another man. It was in the drama of the Restoration and the early eighteenth century, however, that the problem of enforced betrothal received its most developed literary presentation and in such a way as to suggest the first part of Richardson's novel. Only in the drama appeared the same major and minor character types, the same relationships, and even the same scenes as were to appear in the novelist's work.

Edward Ravenscroft's *The Careless Lovers,* a light, unimpressive comedy produced in 1673, presents the story of a tyrannical father, Muchworth, who tries to force his daughter, Jacinta, to marry the conceited coxcomb, De Boastado. His niece and ward, Hillaria, is a gay, outspoken lady who defends and helps her cousin.[19] Certainly these characters in their general situation, in their relationships to one another, and in certain aspects of their personalities are similar to John Harlowe, his daughter Clarissa, Mr. Solmes, and Anna Howe.

The same pattern of figures appears in Charles Hopkins' *Neglected Virtue; or, The Unhappy Conquerour,* produced in 1695.[20] Curio warns his brother, Bretton, not to force his fourteen-year-old daughter, Amadine, into a marriage she does not desire. But Bretton is not a kindly man and tells his daughter, in a scene quite similar to several in *Clarissa,* that she must marry whom he chooses. In the scene in the play and those in the novel there seem to be the same tyrannical father and oppressed daughter experiencing the very same confrontation:

> *Bret.* You know my Mind, therefore let me see you study to deserve it.
> *Am.* I shall endeavor to obey you. But noble Sir—
> *Bret.* Hold your Peace, you little Ferret you, let me have none of your set Phrases. (I, i)

> Hope nothing. Tell me [John Harlowe] not of *hopes,* but of *facts.* I ask nothing of you but what is in your *power* to comply with, and what it is your *duty* to comply with.

> Then sir, I [Clarissa] *will* comply with it;—But yet
> I hope from your goodness—
>   No expostulations! No *but's,* girl! No qualifyings!
> I will be obeyed.   (I, 53)

Amadine is defended vehemently by her cousin Ariena, as is
Clarissa by Anna Howe. But Ariena's assistance is to no avail.
Bretton chooses the ignorant coxcomb Castilio for his daughter's
husband because he is the grandson and heir of a wealthy man,
and the marriage will bring financial advantage to both families.
Castilio, "new-comb'd and powder'd, like a Prentice upon a
Holy-day," visits Amadine and explains to her that he expects
to obtain "A good Estate, with the Tail tagg'd to it" from their
marriage. Amadine chooses the only possible solution to her
dilemma by fleeing with her love, Lycastes. By the end of the
drama they are married and reconciled to Bretton. Hopkins'
characters are more developed than those in Ravenscroft's play
and bear stronger resemblances to the figures in Richardson's
work. Bretton and Clarissa's father are more tyrannical than
Muchworth and would more readily sacrifice their daughters'
happiness for large marriage settlements. Both Castilio and
Solmes are immoral, selfish, and repulsive creatures who would
force themselves upon the poor heroines. Amadine is as innocent as Jacinta, but possesses the courage and sensibility of
Clarissa. The role of the outspoken friend also is more fully
developed by Hopkins and Richardson than by the author of
The Careless Lovers.

Another interesting treatment of the enforced-betrothal
theme appeared in 1722 in John Sturmy's *The Compromise; or,
Faults on Both Sides.* Sir Lewis Despotick is the tyrannical
father who insists that his daughter, Harriet, marry Coupee, a
man who has been recommended for her husband by Sir Lewis'
brother. But Harriet loves her brother's sensible, moral, and
appropriately named friend, Weighty, whom Despotick dislikes
because of Weighty's political convictions. Like John Harlowe,
the father forbids his daughter to see one suitor and commands
her to receive the attentions of another. Harriet is an intelligent
and virtuous woman and, like Clarissa, is capable of choosing

a mate for herself. She has a witty and sharp-tongued friend, Isabella, the niece of old Despotick's political enemy, Sir Clement Harpye, who is in love with her brother. After some rather flat political satire, Despotick is finally brought to the realization that a man cannot be judged by his politics and grants Weighty permission to marry Harriet. Thus, here again are the types of the virtuous daughter, cruel father, ridiculous suitor, and outspoken female friend.

The resemblances between the first part of *Clarissa* and these plays show the considerable extent to which Richardson was influenced by the drama in his development of the enforced-betrothal theme.[21] He uses the same plot situation and the same character types as the dramatists. He presents these figures in similar scenes and gives them similar speeches. But Richardson, afforded the freedom of the novel, developed these characters into more complicated and credible figures than their prototypes in the drama. The father became more than a comical oppressive tyrant, willing to sacrifice his child's happiness for financial gain or his own whim; he became the family patriarch, the symbol of traditional family authority.[22] But John Harlowe also is human in his needs, demanding filial obedience, desiring his son to obtain a peerage, and seeking to make his "favorite child" a scapegoat for his physical ailment.

Richardson transformed the superficial, oppressed heroine of these plays into a complex woman, developing her personality and detailing with great perception her actions and reactions. Clarissa is not a perfect creature, but is a woman torn by uncertainty and pride. Yet, unlike her counterparts in the drama, she is able to withstand paternal demands, while maintaining loyalty to her family as well as to herself. Richardson portrayed his heroine's plight far more seriously than the playwrights had done; Clarissa is not fighting to marry the man she loves, but is struggling to enforce her human rights in a world dominated by men. She emerges as the new woman of the eighteenth century, fighting for economic survival and demanding respect for the sacredness of her individuality.

Richardson also developed the character of the unwanted suitor. Solmes is a disease that blights the happiness of others, but he also is a human being, real in his selfishness, ignorance, and brutality. Clarissa is not threatened by an innocuous cox-comb whom she might ignore after her marriage to him, but is challenged by a menace to her happiness and independence. In Anna Howe, Richardson again created a woman far more sympathetic and complex than her prototypes in the drama. Hillaria, Ariena, and Isabella are quick-witted, outspoken, and, at times, even rude and flirtatious, but they are superficial comic figures, amusing in their wit and repartee, and function-ing in the plots primarily as confidantes and contrasts to the serious heroines. Richardson gave Anna not only the attributes of these gay ladies but also an intelligence and an impressive capacity for friendship. Most important, Richardson portrayed Anna in her own personal world and as a character with ambiv-alent relationships with her mother and suitor.

Clarissa, with her immaculate virtue, white garments, and pale features, and Lovelace, with his sexual lust and impassioned behavior, are embodiments of the archetypal figures of the angelic woman and the demoniac man. In literature these archetypes often are involved in an act of sexual defilement. Because the forced sex act is a gross violation of the dignity of woman and is a form of spiritual murder, it generally results in some kind of death: Prosperina goes to the underworld, Philomela is changed into a nightingale, Lucrece commits sui-cide, and Clarissa's soul rapidly makes its way to heaven. But Richardson's heroine and villain also are products of their own age.[23] Clarissa is a creation of English middle-class puritan sensibility, and Lovelace is an eighteenth-century rake. Both of their character types frequently appeared in Restoration and eighteenth-century drama.

The second part of *Clarissa* is tragic in plot and treatment and can be related to tragic plays of the period. In this novel, unlike *Pamela,* the rape is performed, and moral, social, and economic attitudes of the day demanded that a ruined woman be treated as a tragic figure.[24] Clarissa is a type of heroine common in the tragedies of the period, a heroine who suffered much, often to maintain her virtue. In the excellence of her nature, the importance of her virtue, the strength of her dignity, and in the intensity of her agony, Clarissa is closely related to these heroines of the theater.[25] A discussion of only a few of these dramatic figures will show their influence upon Richardson's heroine.

An early example of such a character appears in John Banks' *Vertue Betray'd; or, Anna Bullen* (1682). Anna has been forced to marry King Henry against her will. Now trapped in a plot against her life, she shows the same type of virtuous and suffering behavior as Clarissa:

> *Queen.* Oh Brother! plead no more, 'tis all in vain;
> Do not betray thy Sister to a Guilt,
> And stain the Crystal Virtue of a Soul,
> Which still she holds far dearer than a Crown.
>
> (IV, i)

Both Anna and Clarissa are forced into relationships with selfish and unattractive men, though the former marries her undesired suitor; both heroines are offered relief in relationships with other men; and both with much pathos and declamation struggle to maintain virtue and dignity, only to be ultimately destroyed.

Rowe's *The Tragedy of Jane Shore* (1714) presents a heroine with even greater resemblances to Clarissa. Richardson was familiar with Rowe's works and probably knew this play, which was very popular throughout the eighteenth century. Like Clarissa, the pathetic heroine of this drama is moral, suffering, and tragic. Jane, formerly mistress to Edward IV, repents of her past actions, as does Richardson's heroine after her rape. Jane and Clarissa must struggle for survival in a male-dominated world:

> *J. Sh:* Such is the Fate unhappy Women find,
> And such the Curse intail'd upon our kind,
> That Man, the lawless Libertine may rove,
> Free and unquestion'd through the Wilds of Love.
>
> (I, ii)

Both women merely desire a retreat in the country, away from the world of men. Jane is offered Hastings' help, as Clarissa is offered that of Lovelace, but she repels his advances, as Richardson's heroine repels those of her assailant. Later Jane refuses to turn against Edward's sons, though her refusal means her destruction. Both Jane and Clarissa eventually die for their virtue. Although the plots of the play and the novel are not very similar, the basic situation of the women martyred for the cause of virtue and a type of superior and suffering heroine are common to both.

The heroine and her predicament in *Marina* (1738), written by George Lillo, also are similar to Clarissa and her plight. *Marina,* based on Shakespeare's *Pericles, Prince of Tyre,* is in Lillo's excessively sentimental style. Although the play ends happily, it has many of the elements of the tragedies related to *Clarissa.* The scenes of particular interest to this study are those in which the virgin heroine is trapped in a house of prostitution. The difficult experiences that Marina has with a bawd, Mother Coupler of Ephesus, are reminiscent of Clarissa's harsh encounters with Mrs. Sinclair:

> *Mar.* The gracious Gods defend me.
> *Bawd.* What, do you offer to say your prayers in my hearing! Is this a place to pray in? Don't provoke me, don't. I find I shall have something to do with you. But you shall bend or break, I can tell you that for your comfort. (I, ii)

Mother Coupler orders Marina to receive several visitors, but, as we are told later, the heroine's tears, prayers, and pleading save her. The maiden then rapidly and efficiently converts to morality and sexual propriety the governor's son, Lysimachus, whom she eventually marries. *Marina* is an inept drama, which attempts to interest the audience largely through the sensational presentation of the scenes in the bawdy house. But the fact that Marina is a spotless virgin imprisoned in a house of prostitution, which is managed by a ruthless bawd, suggests the play's relationship to *Clarissa,* though the ultimate fates of the heroines are quite different. Lillo's work, along with Charles

Johnson's *Caelia,* shows that this dramatic situation had been treated by two of the period's leading playwrights before Richardson began to write his novel.

Anthony Brown's *The Fatal Retirement* (1739) also portrays a heroine who bears resemblance to Clarissa. Pravamor has raped Leonora and attempts to have Artamon blamed for the crime. But Leonora overhears Pravamor talking to an accomplice and discovers the identity of her assailant. Careless of her own safety, she accuses Pravamor, who then murders her. The villain ultimately is killed by the girl's fiancé, Lanertes. Leonora's rape, guilt, shame, and self-willed destruction suggest her relationship to Richardson's heroine. Like Clarissa, she is a violated but virtuous woman who suffers in spite of her strength and, though blameless, feels guilt for her defilement.

It is evident, then, that Clarissa's type of character and situation were not new to the literature of Richardson's day. Tragedies of the Restoration and early eighteenth century often presented the struggles of this type of heroine against the forces of evil for five entire acts. Anna Bullen, Jane Shore, and Leonora fight hopelessly to survive in a world dominated by lustful men. Their efforts to maintain physical and spiritual dignity go for naught, and they are sacrificed to the gods of passion and brutishness. Monimia in Otway's *The Orphan* (1680) and Belvidera in his *Venice Preserv'd* (1682), Isabella in Southerne's *The Fatal Marriage* (1694), and Maria in Hewitt's *Fatal Falsehood* (1734), although placed in circumstances different from those in which Clarissa finds herself, also are tragic figures comparable to Richardson's heroine: like the latter, they are proud and independent women with excessively high standards of morality and a propensity for suffering and emotionalizing.

Richardson wrote to Hill, "I am a good deal warped by the Character of a Gentleman I had in my Eye, when I drew both him [Lovelace], and Mr. B. in Pamela. The best of that Gentleman, for the latter; the worst of him for Lovelace, made still worse by mingling the worst of two other Characters, that were as well known to me, of that Gentleman's Acquaintance."[26] But Lovelace's character type was popular in the theater. The

very name of Lovelace seems derived from the names of such
rakes in the drama as Loveless in *Love's Last Shift* and Wronglove in *Caelia*. The intriguing libertine appeared in comedies
in which he committed his rakish actions and with little change
of attitude still won the heroine; he appeared in other comedies
in which he was converted without too much difficulty from
his evil ways; and he also was a more threatening character in a
darker group of plays. Mr. B. is most closely related to those
libertines in the second group, but Lovelace to those in the
third. The libertines of the darker plays are basically more evil
than those related to Mr. B. Alberto in Thomas Southerne's
The Disappointment; or, The Mother in Fashion (1684) is
such a precursor of Richardson's Lovelace. Alberto, an active
man, is attempting to have a love affair with Alphonso's wife,
Erminia, and also trying to seduce Roger's innocent daughter,
Angelline. He already has seduced Juliana. Alberto has the
same selfish and cynical philosophy about women as Lovelace:

> *Alb.* . . . I've made
> A study of the Sex, and found it frail:
> The black, the brown, the fair, the old, the young,
> Are earthly-minded all: There's not a she,
> The coldest constitution of the Sex,
> Nay, at the Alter, telling o're her Beads,
> But some one rises on her heavenly thoughts,
> That drives her down the wind of strong desire,
> And makes her tast mortality agen.   (I, i)

> "Thou knowest, that I [Lovelace] have more than
> once, twice, or thrice, put to the fiery Trial young
> women of Name and Character; and never yet met
> with one who held out a month; nor indeed so long as
> could puzzle my invention. I have concluded against
> the whole Sex upon it."   (III, 91)

But the play is not a tragedy, and Alberto, after causing much
mischief, finally is converted by Juliana's constancy. Both
Alberto and Lovelace are libertines who desire to seduce as
many pure women as possible to satisfy their own egos and lusts;
both go to unnatural extremes to achieve their victories over

the female sex; and both have a demonic energy and power.

Lothario in Rowe's *The Fair Penitent* also is related to Lovelace. Lothario had seduced Calista before her recent marriage to his enemy, Altamont. Lothario feels no sorrow for what he has done and plots only for the destruction of his enemy. He meets with Calista, but her husband discovers them and promptly kills him in a duel. The similarities between Lothario and Lovelace have been noted: Dr. Johnson first suggested that Richardson in his portrayal of Lovelace was influenced by Rowe's character; and H. G. Ward, in 1912, attempted to prove this indebtedness.[27] Richardson quotes *The Fair Penitent* in his correspondence and twice in *Clarissa*. He has Belford in *Clarissa* compare Calista and Lothario with Clarissa and Lovelace—the point is even made that "Lothario, 'tis true, seems such another wicked ungenerous varlet as thou knowest who: The author knew how to draw a Rake" (VII, 133). As Ward points out, both villains are proud noblemen and scorners of marriage. In possessing the heroines sexually they are partly motivated by their desire to punish their victims' families for refusing them as suitors, and both die for carrying out their revenge. But Lothario appears too seldom in the play to be sufficiently developed as a figure upon which Lovelace might be based. Nevertheless, Lothario is one of the characters in the tradition to which Lovelace belongs, and certainly had some effect upon Richardson's conception of his villain. In his few moments on the stage Lothario displays a dark playfulness and delight in intrigue that undoubtedly influenced Richardson's portrayal of Lovelace.

The novelist probably knew Theophilus Cibber's *The Lover* (1731), particularly since its author was the son of his friend Colley Cibber. The play presents another interesting specimen of the rake. Prompted by greed and lust, Granger wishes to wed Inanthe. He has a ward, Laetitia, whom he already has ruined. Granger, like Lovelace, justifies his behavior by the desire for variety in sex:

> *Gran.* Poor Devil! love thee! what, after ten
> Years Possession! Unconscionable Baggage! She was a

lovely Creature when first I knew her—I think in her blooming Fifteen, as fresh and fragrant as a new-bloom Rose: But what of that? who the devil cou'd eat Ortilans for ever?—how insipid were this Life without Variety? (II, ii)

Lovelace. And yet the Sex do not consider, that Variety and Novelty give the Ardour and the Obsequiousness; and that, were the Rake as much used to them as the Husband is, he would be and is to *his own Wife,* if married *as* indifferent to their favours, as their Husbands are. (IV, 134)

Granger, like Lovelace, is able to appear moral in order to further his designs. But when Inanthe tests her suitors by informing them that her father has lost his fortune, Granger reverts to true villainous form by sending her a note in which he promises to support her if she will be his mistress. Both Granger and Lovelace are skillful actors, capable of appearing moral and sincere in the presence of their female victims; both frequently are driven to evil acts by their desire for sexual conquest; and both consider all women as existing only to satisfy the desires of men. Although Cibber's villain does not possess the charm and fascination of Lovelace, he resembles him in his dark qualities and in his base treatment of women.

The character of the rake was scarcely as developed in the fiction of the period as in the theater—indeed, in such novels as Mrs. Davys' *The Accomplish'd Rake; or, Modern Fine Gentleman* (1727) in which he did appear, he seems to have been a weak imitation of his dramatic counterpart. In the preface to her novel, Mrs. Davys suggests that her work is much in debt to the drama, but her protagonist, Sir John, certainly has little of the vividness, energy, and specific character traits of Lovelace and the dramatic rakes. The novel itself is a weak assortment of sensational episodes.[28] Though actual rakes occasionally were discussed in such periodical essays as *Spectator* Nos. 75 and 152, both by Steele, they were not given developed characterizations, nor do they much resemble Richardson's villain. In the former essay Steele discusses the cursing of libertines, a fault from which

Lovelace is free, and in the latter essay he analyzes in general terms the passion for pleasure which overcomes these men.[29]

Unquestionably Lovelace most resembles the evil libertines of the drama. Like these villains, he is motivated by sexual desire and contempt for women. Like them, he is a diabolical deceiver who displays great energy and a sardonic sense of humor in his intrigues. Lovelace possesses the same egotism, the same inflated image of himself as these libertines of the drama. But despite the influence that such figures had on his characterization, Lovelace is a strikingly original and complex portrayal. He is morally corrupt in his romantic attachments but honest in his affairs with men. His need to triumph over women makes him facile at intrigue and deception, yet compelling and attractive in the excitement he generates. Richardson's rake is the finest and most subtle portrayal of a character type that had been developed in the English drama.

Of all the plays of this period, none bears so striking a resemblance to *Clarissa* as Charles Johnson's *Caelia; or, The Perjur'd Lover*. The play was not successful, probably because of the sensationalism of certain scenes and the harsh realism of its story.[30] Johnson was a well-known playwright who had written a large group of plays, two of which were performed frequently.[31] Hence, it is difficult to believe that Richardson was not familiar with Johnson's works and aware of *Caelia*. Bernbaum, McKillop, and Nicoll have noticed the play's similarities to the novel, but no examination of this relationship has yet appeared.[32]

The plot of Johnson's drama is concerned with Caelia's elopement with Wronglove, his subsequent desertion, and her death. At the beginning of the work Bellamy, a friend of the heroine and villain, is informed of the elopement by Meanwell, a servant of Caelia's father. Caelia, he is told, is now pregnant and due to have the child in three months. Bellamy then presents the theme of the entire play in terms that suggest a passage written by Belford, his counterpart in Richardson's novel. Bellamy and Belford, clearly speaking for their authors, condemn the gentlemen of their time who delight in ruining innocent young women:

> *Bell.* I will tell thee, honest *Meanwell*: there is not one thing above Ground so void of any sense of Shame, or Vertue, as a young Whoremaster—but one Passion governs—I know not how it comes to be so, but this Practice of ruining young innocent Girls, is look'd on only as a Piece of Galantry—as part of a Gentleman's Accomplishments. (I, i)

> [*Belford.*] *Man* acting thus by *man,* we should not be at a loss to give such actions a name: But is it not doubly and trebly aggravated, when such advantage is taken of an unexperienced and innocent young creature, whom we pretend to love above all the women in the world; and when we seal our pretences by the most solemn vows and protestations of inviolable honour, that we can invent? (VII, 316)

In the following scene, between the heroine and the villain, it becomes evident that Wronglove has promised Caelia marriage and now pretends to make arrangements for a reconciliation with her father. But meanwhile he has taken lodgings for her:

> *Wrong.* At a good sort of an old Woman's; one Mrs. Lupine's, a Midwife—Oh, 'tis a very handsome House, there are none but People of Condition live in the Street—She will make Preparations for you against the good Hour. (I, ii)

Clarissa also is deceived about lodgings and, like Caelia, lured to a house of prostitution:

> You may have good accommodations in Dover-street, at a widow's. . . .
> . . . she is very careful, she says, that she takes no Lodgers, but of *figure* and *reputation*. She rents two good houses, . . . joined by a *large handsome passage*.

> The *inner-house* is the genteelest, and is very elegantly
> furnished.   (III, 194)

Mrs. Lupine, the proprietress of the establishment in which
Caelia is to live, soon arrives; she is as wicked and vulgar as
Mrs. Sinclair, her counterpart in Richardson's novel. It becomes
obvious to the reader, though not to the poor heroine, that this
woman is in charge of a brothel. Caelia leaves with her, and
Wronglove discusses his motive for seducing the heroine in a
brief soliloquy that bears similarity to many speeches uttered by
Lovelace. Both villains are fond of depicting their love affairs
as "chases," and both seem more delighted with intrigue than
with actual conquest:

> *Wrong.*   But I am fond of the Sport, so delighted
> with the Chace—If I cou'd eat as heartily as I can hunt
> the Venison, the Girls and I shou'd agree well enough.
>   (I, ii)

> *Lovelace.*   By all this, seest thou not, how greatly
> preferable it is, on twenty accounts, to pursue a diffi-
> cult, rather than an easy chace? . . .
> Thou knowest nothing, Jack, of the delicacies of
> intrigue; Nothing of the glory of outwitting the Witty
> and the Watchful: Of the joys that fill the mind of
> the inventive or contriving genius.   (III, 77)

Once in her new lodgings the heroine is shocked by the
behavior and manner of Mrs. Lupine. Caelia learns the nature
of her abode and discovers that she is only one of several women
whom Wronglove has deserted in this disreputable place. One
is reminded of Mrs. Sinclair's house in *Clarissa* and such women
as Sally and Polly, whom Lovelace had corrupted and then
settled there. Mrs. Lupine gives Caelia a letter from Wronglove
in which the libertine states that his father has arranged
another marriage for him. Meanwell soon arrives, promises to
help Caelia, and leaves to find new lodgings for her. But the
girl is arrested and taken to jail with the other inhabitants of
Mrs. Lupine's house.

The last act of the play takes place primarily in the poorly furnished room that is the heroine's prison. Caelia talks to the keeper's wife and tells her, "I have no Friend, Relation, or Acquaintance, indeed I have none." Her entire scene with the woman is strikingly similar to Clarissa's scene with the officer in whose house she is held prisoner. Each heroine, in a pathetic manner, foresees her death and offers a ring to the person she addresses:

> *Caelia.* See me decently laid in Earth, at Night, in a plain coffin; in the Church of this Parish—Enquire not into my Family, my Name, or Story. And please to accept, and keep this Ring, in Memory of your Charity and Goodness to an unhappy Creature. (V, i)

> I [Clarissa] will die with you, and in this very corner. And you shall be well satisfied for the trouble you have had with me.—I have value enough for that —for, see, I have a diamond ring; taking it out of her bosom; and I have friends will redeem it at a high price, when I am gone.   (VI, 301)

In a later scene (V, iii) Caelia regrets her guilt, much as Clarissa will do after her ravishment (V, 329). The heroine's father, Lovemore, enters and participates with his daughter in a touching scene. Lovemore forgives his daughter, but she feels unworthy of his kindness and faints. A gentleman arrives and announces that Bellamy, avenging Caelia, has killed Wronglove in a duel. Wronglove has died saying, *"Bellamy is a Man of Honour; I provoked him to what has happened;* I struck him." His dying statement is similar to that uttered by Lovelace: "But be ye all witnesses that I have provoked my destiny, and acknowledge, that I fall by a Man of Honour" (VIII, 275). Before Wronglove died he had written a note in which he leaves all his property to Caelia and asks his father to protect her and the child. The shock is too much for the heroine. She dies, asking only to be buried in her mother's grave.

Written by one of the period's well-known playwrights sixteen years before the publication of *Clarissa, Caelia* bears significant similarities to Richardson's novel. The heroines of both works resemble each other in personality and situation.

Caelia, however, has succumbed sexually to Wronglove before the action of the play, but her penitence and suffering evoke forgiveness even from her father. By the end of the novel Clarissa too has lost her virginity, and she also expiates her guilt through repentance. Both heroines run away from home with their suitors, are brought to London by these villains, and are tricked into brothels. Both eventually are arrested and imprisoned and die soon after. The libertines who ruin these heroines also have much in common: Wronglove and Lovelace are selfish members of the upper class, concerned primarily with satisfying their desires; both see the female sex as existing only for their enjoyment; both intrigue and destroy without concern for their victims' welfare; and both die in duels, aware of the evil they have performed and forgiving their executioners. Each villain has a friend who is converted from his moral laxity by the plight of the heroine and who tries unsuccessfully to help her. Bellamy loved Caelia before she eloped with Wronglove; Belford first meets Clarissa after her flight from home with Lovelace and immediately seems to fall in love with her. Bellamy, however, avenges the heroine by killing the villain in a duel, and thus performs the role of Morden in the novel. Finally, the bawds and prostitutes in both works also are remarkably similar. Mrs. Lupine and Mrs. Sinclair are vulgar and completely immoral creatures, and the females who work for them are lewd women who have been corrupted by deceiving men.

Caelia and the second part of *Clarissa* expose the same social problem: Johnson and Richardson, aware of the ruin suffered by a woman who has lost her chastity, show the inherent immorality of the masculine code of conduct, which required a man to behave with honor and dignity in all matters except love. The playwright and the novelist, exposing this social problem of their time and displaying sympathy for its victims, also created works similar in emphasis and tone; *Caelia* and *Clarissa* are sentimental tragedies because of the abundance of tearful and pathetic emotions used to develop their moral themes.

Caelia probably suggested the second part of *Clarissa* to

Richardson. The two works resemble each other not only in theme, plot, and major characters but also in such similar details as the presentation by each heroine of a ring to one of her jailers, such similar lines as those uttered by the dying villains, and such similar secondary figures as the villains' morally converted friends. But such an influence scarcely diminishes Richardson's achievement—the wonder is that he developed the relatively limited material of the play into his monumental novel.

Although the heroes and heroines of the heroic tragedy of the Restoration were high in social standing and were placed in uncommon predicaments, these figures did have some effect upon Richardson's portrayal of his heroine and villain.[33] The main subject of the heroic tragedy generally was love, and these plays gave much attention to the passions of their characters. Emotions were depicted in a greatly exaggerated manner and the playwrights, striving for high dramatic effect, developed a type of ranting rhetoric.[34] Certainly Clarissa and Lovelace exhibit extreme passions in a more pronounced manner and with a more unnatural rhetoric than the characters of the plays previously discussed in this chapter. Examine the following brief sections from the penknife scene in *Clarissa*:

> She turned to me: "Stop where thou art, O vilest and most abandoned of men!—Stop where thou art!— Nor, with that determined face, offer to touch me, if thou wouldst not that I should be a corpse at thy feet!"
> To my astonishment, she held forth a penknife in her hand, the point to her own bosom, grasping resolutely the whole handle, so that there was no offering to take it from her.
>
> .   .   .   .   .
>
> She withdrew to the door, and set her back against it, holding the pointed knife to her heaving bosom; while the women held me, beseeching me not to provoke the violent Lady. . . . While the truly-heroic Lady braved me, at that distance:

> "Approach me, Lovelace, with resentment, if thou
> wilt. I dare die. It is in defence of my Honour. God
> will be merciful to my poor Soul! I expect no mercy
> from thee! I have gained this distance, and two steps
> nearer me, and thou shalt see what I dare do!—"
>
> Leave me, women, to myself, and to my angel!—
> They retired at a distance—O my beloved creature,
> how you terrify me—Holding out my arms, and kneel-
> ing on one knee—Not a step, not a step farther, except
> to receive my death at that injured hand which is thus
> held up against a life far dearer to me than my own!
> I am a villain! the blackest of villains!—Say you will
> sheath your knife in the injurer's, not the injured's
> heart; and then will I indeed approach you, but not
> else.   (VI, 67-69)

The dialogue is inflated and highly theatrical, the stances of
the characters are melodramatic, and their passions unnatural.
It is obvious that Richardson is presenting his figures in the
same exaggerated and artificial heroic manner as did, for
example, Dryden and Lee. This is not the pathetic Clarissa,
but rather a heroicizing Clarissa, a ranting and raving Clarissa;
and this is not the plotting, intriguing Lovelace, but an overcome and frenzied Lovelace. Both characters seem to be
posturing, rather than behaving realistically.

The source of this behavior is suggested several times in the
novel itself when Lovelace quotes from heroic tragedies to
describe and even heighten his own mood and thoughts. For
example, to describe his strong feelings for Clarissa he uses
the inflated language of Alexander in Lee's *The Rival Queens*
(1677, III, i): *"O ecstasy!—My heart will burst my breast, / To
leap into her bosom!—"* (III, 1); and to express his horror at
her death he borrows a few lines from Ziphares in Lee's *Mithri-
dates* (1678, V, ii): *"She's out! The damp of death has quench'd
her quite! / Those spicy doors, her lips, are shut, close lock'd, /
Which never gale of life shall open more!"* (VIII, 51).[35]

Exaggerated heroic qualities often irritate the reader and
destroy for him the characters' credibility. But when such
qualities are controlled by other aspects of characterization,

46

and as a result are toned down, when Clarissa and Lovelace act and speak with less exaggeration, but with the same force and power as the supermen and superwomen of the heroic tragedy, they achieve a unique vitality and reality. Such scenes demonstrate how a writer can be influenced without losing his originality and how he can reshape the materials of lesser art into his own more striking creation. For certainly there is a basic drive, a strength of will, and an individualism in Richardson's characters that were at least in part the result of the heroic tragedy, and certainly these elements helped to make the heroine and villain the most dynamic, fascinating, and compelling figures yet to appear in prose fiction.

Richardson was able to make use of traditional dramatic elements and yet combine them into his original portrayals. In the following excerpts Richardson uses the stock dramatic figures of the suffering virgin and evil rake, blending in them character elements from the heroic tragedy and she-tragedy and bringing the heroine and villain to life with his own realism of character and presentation:

> She wrung her hands. She disordered her head-dress. She tore her ruffles. She was in a perfect phrensy.
> I dreaded her returning malady: But entreaty rather exasperating, I affected an angry air.—I bid her expect the worst she had to fear—And was menacing on, in hopes to intimidate her, when, dropping down at my feet,
> 'Twill be a mercy, said she, the highest act of mercy you can do, to kill me outright upon this spot.
>
> . . . . .
>
> Nay, if I must not touch you; for she wildly slapt my hands; but with such a sweet passionate Air, her bosom heaving and throbbing as she looked up to me, that altho' I was most sincerely enraged, I could with transport have pressed her to mine.
> If I must not touch you, I will not.—But depend upon it [and I assumed the sternest air I could assume, to try what *that* would do], depend upon it, Madam, that this is not the way to avoid the evils you dread.

47

. . . . .

. . . snatching up hastily her head from the chair, and as hastily popping it down again in terror, [she] hit her nose, I suppose, against the edge of the chair; and it gushed out with blood, running in a stream down her bosom; she herself too much affrighted to heed it.

Never was mortal man in such a terror and agitation as I; for I instantly concluded, that she had stabbed herself with some concealed instrument.

I ran to her in a wild agony—For Dorcas was frighted out of all her mock interposition—

What have you done!—O what have you done!— Look up to me, my dearest life!—Sweet injured inno- cence, look up to me: What have you done!—Long will I not survive you!—And I was upon the point of draw- ing my sword to dispatch myself, when I discovered— [what an unmanly blockhead does this charming creature make me at her pleasure!] that all I appre- hended was but a bloody nose, which, as far as I know (for it could not be stopped in a quarter of an hour), may have saved her head and her intellects.

(V, 375-78)

Sir Charles Grandison contains two distinct levels of action: the first deals with the hero's relationship with Harriet; and the second with his unhappy association with Clementina. Since the story of Sir Charles and Harriet emphasizes everyday social behavior and lacks a major action, it has little connection with standard literary plots of the period. The story of Sir Charles and Clementina has considerably more dramatic action, but I have been unable to find any literary sources for its plot and for the Italian characters, apart from Clementina, whose mad behavior was apparently suggested to Richardson by Shakespeare's Ophelia. McKillop states that the "Italian back- ground was probably worked out with the aid of Giuseppi Baretti, a literary adventurer who had come to London in 1751 and who undoubtedly made Richardson's acquaintance through Samuel Johnson."[36]

But many of the characters that appear in the story of Sir Charles and Harriet can be related to the drama of the period. The hero himself is an elaborate portrayal of the drama's man of sense. This figure, as Professor Smith has demonstrated, was a popular dramatic type of the period.[37] In part a reaction to the Dorimants and Horners—much as Sir Charles is in part a reaction to Tom Jones—this dramatic figure was a paragon of virtue and something of a prig. The man of sense is not to be found as a character type either in the essay or in earlier fiction.[38] It was Richardson's friend Colley Cibber who in his play *The Lady's Last Stake; or, the Wife's Resentment,* presented what is probably the first full portrayal of this figure. Sir Friendly Moral is described by Lord Wronglove as a man who "is as good humour'd, and as well bred, as if he had no Principles at all" (III, i). Sir Friendly's main function in the work is to reunite Lord Wronglove and his wife after their marital difficulties. Throughout the work he does little more than advise and preach morality. But the best known of these dramatic characters during the period, and the figure closest to Richardson's Sir Charles, is Bevil Junior in Steele's *The Conscious Lovers* (1722).[39] Early in the work this character explains his motives for doing good: "If Pleasure be worth purchasing, how great a Pleasure is it to him, who has a true Taste of Life, to ease an Aking Heart. . . . This is the Effect of an humane Disposition, where there is only a general Tye of Nature, and common Necessity. What then must it be, when we serve an Object of Merit, of Admiration!" (II, ii). He later declines a duel because of his moral convictions and delivers a speech on the subject similar to one uttered by Sir Charles:

> *Bev. jun.*   But, Sir, you know, I have often dared to disapprove of the Decisions a Tyrant Custom has introduc'd, to the Breach of all Laws, both Divine and Human.   (IV, i)

There are many bad customs, Mr. Reeves, that I [Sir Charles] grieve for: But for none so much as this of premeditated duelling. Where is the magnanimity of the man that cannot get above the vulgar breath?

49

... A man who defies his fellow-creature into the field,
into a private quarrel, must first defy his God.

(I, 316)

Steele's hero is a direct precursor of Sir Charles Grandison.
He has the same virtuous soul and moral dislike for dueling.
Bevil Junior and Sir Charles are exemplary heroes. Both are
keenly aware of the troubles that beset less fortunate beings,
and both devote a considerable portion of their time to helping
those in distress. In their great respect for their parents and in
their exaggerated politeness to women, Bevil Junior and Sir
Charles contrast sharply with many of the heroes of the earlier
drama and novel. They are well-mannered young men who
possess an unnatural control over their passions and who seem
in complete harmony with the universe. The dramatic situations of both men are also similar: like Sir Charles, Bevil
Junior is in love with a woman he has saved from abduction,
but is morally committed to marry another. Vermoil in Fielding's
The Temple Beau (1730), Gaywit in his *The Modern Husband*
(1732), Eustace in Theophilus Cibber's *The Lover*, Bellamy in
Dr. Benjamin Hoadly's *The Suspicious Husband* (1747), and
Lewson in Moore's *The Gamester* (1747) are several more of
the exemplary men in the drama prefiguring Sir Charles.

John Harrington Smith has studied the men of sense that
appeared in the drama after 1700 and has described their
remarkably similar personalities.[40] Each of the qualities that
Professor Smith finds in these figures can also be found in Sir
Charles Grandison. For example, both the drama's man of
sense and Sir Charles are "distinguished by regularity" in their
conduct. Richardson states in his Preface to *Sir Charles Grandison* that his hero is portrayed as an "Example of a Man acting
uniformly well through a Variety of trying Scenes, because
all his Actions are regulated by one steady Principle" (I, viii).
Professor Smith also points out that this type of dramatic hero
is sincere and constant in love matters. Much of Richardson's
novel is devoted to the admirable behavior of Sir Charles in
his romances with Clementina and Harriet; unlike the hero of
the comedy of manners, Sir Charles is neither dishonest nor

flippant in his love affairs. According to Professor Smith, "the true man of sense is more cool than his prototype in tragi-comedy, and in him the tender passion loses some of its transports"; moreover, his manner of courtship "is the more likely to be well received if not marked by 'modish gallantry.' " Sir Charles courts Harriet and even proposes to her in a calm, reasonable, and controlled manner. And like this dramatic type, Sir Charles adopts "a tone of condescension towards his less well governed fellowmen," but he "makes a point of toler-ating their weaknesses."

Richardson does not improve upon the men of sense of the drama, but presents their shortcomings in his own portrayal of Sir Charles, who also is annoying and unnatural in his con-sistently noble behavior and discourse. At the same time, Sir Charles is never threatened by a difficult circumstance, nor does he seem capable of deep feeling. His sensibility responds to the admirable behavior and noble feelings of others, but no experience of his own causes him to suffer or react with passion. His reserve, decorum, and manners form a solid wall between him and the reader. The fact that Sir Charles writes few letters is indicative of his superficial character. The epistle had become for Richardson's major figures an instrument of self-revelation, and what inner self could such a hero have?

It is difficult to suggest definite precursors for Harriet Byron; she might have developed from any of the countless and indistinct dramatic heroines of the time.[41] Richardson does at times successfully portray her female nature, for in certain of her letters he presents her womanly preoccupations, qualms, wit, and garrulity with great skill. But in much of the work she reveals herself as little more than a love-sick female waiting to be claimed by her hero.

Sir Charles' sister, Charlotte Grandison, is a character of greater interest. She is intelligent, sharp-witted, and talkative, with some charm and a certain amount of good will. In her merry behavior, her love of repartee, and her tendency to be shocking in conversation, she is clearly a product of the gay lady of the drama. This character type appeared frequently in the Restoration and eighteenth-century theater, often as a heroine. But Charlotte is related to those gay ladies of the drama who were too comic to be leading figures and functioned as antithesis to the more gentle heroines. Charlotte's ancestry in the drama is the same as that of Lady Davers and Anna Howe; but Lady Davers is older and more waspish, and Anna is more attractive and slightly more subdued. Many of these gay ladies of the drama of the period have suitors whom they abuse, just as Sir Charles' sister mistreats Lord G.[42] The gay lady and her suitor were purely dramatic figures; they were not established types in the essay or in earlier novels.

Miranda in Catherine Trotter's *Love at a Loss; or, Most Votes Carry It* (1700) has a quick wit and continually abuses her suitor, Constant:

> *Mir.* Well, seriously *Lucilia,* I have been trying this Month to compose my Face for the Wedding-day; for I fancy if one has not a most Reverend Countenance, one will never be thought in earnest at so unreasonable a thing, as taking for better, for worse; it looks so like a jest of stark Madness.
> *Con.* Keep your mad Countenance then, and do it in jest.
> *Mir.* Ay, but that surely one of yours, *Constant,* has such a Husbandly air, 'twill spoil the Jest; I never look upon it but I'm afraid I'm married already.
>
> (II, ii)

Liberia in Gabriel Odingsells' *The Bath Unmask'd* (1725) is another gay lady whose behavior to her suitor is haughty and insulting. Clarinda in the Reverend James Miller's *The Humours of Oxford* (1730) also is a woman of intelligence, wit, and sharp conversation, who treats her lover, Trumore, in an abusive manner. Even more like Charlotte and Lord G. are Rosetta and Colonel Raymond in *The Foundling,* written by Richardson's friend Edward Moore only six years before the publication of *Sir Charles Grandison.* It was produced frequently, and the novelist probably was familiar with it. In *The Foundling* Rosetta refuses to tell Colonel Raymond that she returns his affection for her. She constantly teases and angers him and even feigns interest in a fop named Faddle to make the colonel jealous. Her behavior to the colonel is quite insolent:

> *Col.* And was it so, Madam?—And may I hope?
> *Roset.* Was it so, Madam?—And may I hope?
> *(mocking him)* No, Sir, it was not so—and you may not
> hope.   (I, iii)

But, like Charlotte, Rosetta is slowly won over by the goodness of her wooer.

The relationship between these gay ladies and their suitors of the drama and Charlotte and Lord G. can be suggested by a single citation from the novel:

> What, Sir, am I to be buffeted, Sir?—
> He put his hat under his arm again—*Buffeted,*
> madam!—Would to heaven—
> What has Heaven to do with your odd ways, Lord G.?
> I beg pardon for intruding, madam,—But I thought—
> That you had a privilege, Sir—but marriage itself,
> Sir, shall not give you a privilege to break into my
> retirements. You *thought*, Sir—You could *not think*—
> So much the worse if you did—   (III, 341-42)

This passage is remarkably similar to those from the above plays: here is the same type of bright, cruelly witty, and unsentimental lady triumphing unmercifully in a love game with her serious and hopelessly defeated suitor. In their personalities, in their behavior toward each other, and in their scenes of witty confrontation, Richardson's gay lady and humble suitor seem to step right off the English stage.

Like the major figures, many of the secondary characters in *Sir Charles Grandison* are adapted from standard types in the drama. One scene from the novel will suffice to suggest the relationships between these minor characters and certain dramatic stock portrayals. Early in the work, after she has arrived in London, Harriet dines at the home of Lady Betty Williams. Mr. Walden, an Oxford scholar who is rather opinionated and proud of showing his knowledge, is present at the gathering. The pedant and pretender to learning had often been satirized in the drama: Cimberton in Steele's *The Conscious Lovers* and Haughty in Miller's *The Humours of Oxford* (1730) are examples of this character type and bear strong resemblances to Walden. The scene in the novel includes two other characters of note, Miss Cantillon, who is "very pretty; but visibly proud, affected, and conceited," and Sir Hargrave Pollexfen, the rake and coxcomb. Miss Cantillon calls to mind such blithe and conceited young ladies of the drama as Narcissa in Cibber's *Love's Last Shift* and Lady Fancyfull in Vanbrugh's *The Provok'd Wife* (1697). Sir Hargrave bears resemblance to the rakish figures discussed earlier in the chapter, but he is also a comical fop. Harriet describes his airs:

> He forgets not to pay his respects to himself at every glass; yet does it with a seeming consciousness, as if he would hide a vanity too apparent to be concealed; breaking from it, if he finds himself observed, with an half-careless, yet seemingly dissatisfied air, pretending to have discovered something amiss in himself. This seldom fails to bring him a compliment: Of which he shews himself very sensible, by affectedly disclaiming the merit of it; perhaps with this speech, bowing, with his spread hand on his breast, waving his head to and fro—By my Soul, Madam (or Sir) you do me too much honour.
> (I, 62)

Sir Hargrave's vain, foppish, and comical mannerisms suggest such figures in the drama as Brazen in Farquhar's *The Recruiting Officer* (1706) and Captain Bellamont in Fielding's *The Modern Husband*. Mr. Walden, Miss Barnevelt, Miss Cantillon, and Sir Hargrave are depicted in *Sir Charles Grandison* much as their prototypes are portrayed in the theater. Richardson emphasizes a particular affectation that guides the conduct of each of these minor characters. The comic playwrights of the Restoration motivated most of their figures by a single folly or vice; the sentimental playwrights of the eighteenth century often presented such "humour" characters as contrasts to their people of sense. In this scene in *Sir Charles Grandison* Richardson uses the pretentious learning of Mr. Walden, the conceit of Miss Cantillon, and the vanity of Sir Hargrave as contrasts to the natural wisdom, femininity, and supposed modesty of Harriet. The fact that Richardson satirizes in his minor characters those affectations that were satirized by the comic playwrights of the Restoration and eighteenth century in their minor figures further manifests the close relationship between *Sir Charles Grandison* and the drama.

Perhaps what is most significant here is that many of the plays discussed in this chapter are related to the everyday world of their audiences. Characters belong to contemporary social groups and are concerned with contemporary problems of sex and marriage; actions are probable and within a normal social context. The major figures of the novel were romantic heroes and heroines, adventurers, thieves, and pirates; the action of the novel was concerned primarily with exciting events, intrigue, violence, and sex. In spite of the greater realism that Defoe brought to the novel, his characters are still isolated individuals, existing outside the social framework, and experiencing a large number of unusual adventures. The few works of fiction, such as Thomas Brown's *The Adventures of Lindamira* (1702), which attempted to create an illusion of a more normal world and did present some minor characters adapted from the drama, still featured incredible heroes and heroines and unrealistic situations. But much of the comedy and some of the tragedy of the Restoration and eighteenth century were closer to everyday reality. The drama was, after all, a social ritual; the fiction of the period was a diversion, an excuse for fantasy.

Richardson was not interested in writing diversions; nor, as a respectable businessman, did he want to write plays. He wanted to create a new type of novel, a serious and moral type of novel.[43] To do this he had to adapt the more normal characters and situations of the drama. But Richardson also adapted a particular focus of the drama, a focus that we call sentimental because it highlighted the emotional and moral sensibilities of the characters. It was this sentimentalism, discussed in detail in the next chapter, which allowed Richardson his emotional portrayals and which thus made his characters the most psychologically real that had yet appeared in fiction.

Richardson was thus to make most future novelists realize that the novel should present an image of the everyday world, that it should convince the reader of the social normality of its characters and the probability of its actions. Of equal significance is the fact that Richardson's adaptation of dramatic plots was partly responsible for the important changes he made in the structure of the novel. Earlier fiction generally was episodic and discursive. Richardson's focus upon a single situation in *Pamela* and two related situations in *Clarissa* helped these works achieve a dramatic unity that was to be a major influence on the future development of the novel.

CHAPTER THREE

Sentimental Literature & Static Sensibility

Consciously and consistently Richardson tries to edify the reader by having him feel pity for the moral characters when they suffer and happiness when they prosper.[1] At the same time, he lauds in his works such humanitarian qualities as sympathy, altruism, and benevolence.[2] The moral emotionalism and humanitarianism in his fiction make Richardson the first sentimental novelist and link his works with the sentimental drama of the period.[3] But most important is his detailed presentation of emotion, which brought a new dimension to characterization in the novel. Curiously, scholars have noted only the relationship of Richardson's novels to the general sensibility of the period and have made little attempt to explore this connection with sentimental drama.[4] The neglect may result from the fact that sentimental plays of the late Restoration and early eighteenth century did not form a recognized literary group.[5] Nevertheless, certain important qualities, although sometimes appearing in other kinds of dramas, are so emphasized in these sentimental plays that it would be well to consider such works as a distinct dramatic type.

Because the nature of sentimental literature is somewhat complex and because there are no definitive statements on the subject, it is necessary for this study to establish at least the general qualities of these works which influenced Richardson's novels. Sentimental drama seems to have been in part a reaction to the immorality and amorality of the theater.[6] Although much of Colley Cibber's *Love's Last Shift; or, The Fool in Fashion*

(1696) is like the comedy of manners, the scenes in which Amanda appears are different in substance and tone. The elements of this part of the play make *Love's Last Shift* the first English sentimental comedy and are the very elements that became part of the sentimental movement throughout the eighteenth century. Moral emphasis is the most important of these elements. A song in the masque performed during the last act suggests the lesson to be learned from the play: "Where first I [Love] promis'd thee a happy Life, / There thou shalt find it in a Vertuous Wife." Cibber, through the Amanda-Loveless relationship, wants to show that happiness can be achieved in marriage when both husband and wife are virtuous and have respect for each other. He also wishes to demonstrate, by Amanda's eventual happiness, that virtue always is rewarded. But a moral theme alone does not make a sentimental drama. As Ernest Bernbaum suggests, the audience must also admire virtuous characters and feel strong pity for them when they suffer.[7] Cibber's Amanda certainly elicits these emotions. She is a virtuous and long-suffering wife who has led a lonely existence for eight years while her husband, Loveless, has been living wildly on the continent. All the while she has remained loyal to him and has not forsaken her marriage vows to find pleasure with another man. Amanda thus fulfills a role that will be basic in most sentimental comedies of the eighteenth century: as a virtuous character, she contends against distresses with much suffering, but is "finally rewarded by morally deserved happiness."[8]

Morality and emotionalism often are linked in one other manner in sentimental drama; a villain or even less evil character is led to virtue by an appeal to his emotions. He first feels guilt for his sins, and then joy from his newly found virtue. In the case of *Love's Last Shift* an errant husband returns and experiences an emotional and moral conversion through the realization of his wife's goodness. On discovering Amanda's virtue, Loveless cries, "Oh I am confounded with my guilt, and tremble to behold thee," and a moment later says, "with this tender Grasp of fond reviving Love I seize my Bliss" (V, ii). Loveless seems to be converted to a state of complete virtue through the following emotional sequence: he first feels pity for Amanda's suffering, he then is confounded by shame for his guilt, and he finally begins to know the joys of virtuous behavior. Loveless articulates his new sense of morality with characteristic emotionalism: "Oh thou hast rouz'd me from my deep Lethargy of Vice! For hitherto my Soul has been enslav'd to loose Desires. . . . Thus let me kneel and pay my thanks to her, whose conquering Virtue has at last subdu'd me" (V, ii).

Cibber's *The Careless Husband* also links virtue with tearful sentiment. The audience is called upon to admire Lady Easy for her noble behavior in relation to her husband's infidelity, and to pity her for the suffering she undergoes because of her moral stand.[9] Here again, as in *Love's Last Shift,* the husband is converted to virtue by the pity he feels for his wife upon realizing the grief he has caused her, and by the joy he achieves from his new sense of morality. Such plays as Johnson's *Country Lasses,* Lillo's *Silvia,* and Steele's *The Conscious Lovers* also possess this kind of emotional moralism and thus may be considered sentimental comedies.

The new sensibility found expression in tragedy also, though somewhat more slowly. *The Fatal Extravagance* (1721), by Richardson's close friend, Aaron Hill, is one of the more consistently sentimental tragedies.[10] Bellmour, the hero of this play, is highly virtuous except for his love of gambling, which ultimately causes his destruction. Bernbaum finds that in all sentimental tragedies a virtuous person is overcome by catastrophes for which he is not responsible.[11] But in many of the plays of this type the hero has some flaw or commits some moral error that in part causes the suffering he experiences. The lesson to be learned from Bellmour's behavior is constantly emphasized throughout the work: "Mean, and Ignoble, Pleasures *break* the Mind, / Un-nerve our Judgement, and our Reason blind" (III). Bellmour provides an example of what the sin of gambling can do to a virtuous soul. But his misfortunes are unnecessary in that they are brought about by the machinations of the villain, Bargrave, who takes advantage of his weakness. The audience is called upon to pity a hero who is made to suffer disproportionately for a single flaw and also to condemn the vice that allows him to be destroyed. In *The Fatal Extravagance,* as in most sentimental tragedies, there is also a purely virtuous character who has not sinned, but who suffers from pity for the central character. Louisa through her loyalty to her husband receives much sorrow and is herself almost overcome by the catastrophes that befall him; her characterization is designed to elicit sentimental responses from the audience.

Ten years later George Lillo's *The London Merchant* added significant support to the development of this type of tragedy. The play, suggested by "The Ballad of George Barnwell," is clearly a product of the new sensibility. George is a youth of noble character, but his overwhelming passion for Millwood drives him to crime and eventually destroys him. At the end of the play he is excessively repentant, and his execution is made to seem almost undeserved. George is loved by Maria, a virtuous girl who suffers greatly for him. The abundance of emotion displayed by George and Maria, their admirable behavior during much of the play, and the numerous moral sentiments expressed throughout the work make *The London Merchant* a prime example of sentimental tragedy. The following year another sentimental tragedy appeared: Charles Johnson's *Caelia.*

Certain other qualities characterize sentimental drama. Because the theater audiences in the first part of the eighteenth century were becoming more middle class, and because sentimental drama itself was in part a reaction to the aristocratic libertinism celebrated in the earlier comedy of manners, the new type of play treated common domestic relationships and bourgeois activities more favorably. While Congreve in *Love for Love* (1695) portrays cynically the relationship between Sir Sampson Legend and his son Valentine, Steele in *The Conscious Lovers* treats with sympathy the association between Bevil Senior and Bevil Junior. In Farquhar's *The Constant Couple* (1699) the merchant Smuggler is sharply satirized, whereas in *The Conscious Lovers* old Sealand is drawn with great respect.[12]

At the same time, sentimental tragedy was mostly concerned

with characters lower in the social hierarchy than those in other types of Restoration and early eighteenth-century tragedy. The heroic drama presented aristocratic characters, the tragedy of pathos presented high-ranking figures—although Richardson was to admire Otway's *The Orphan* for its domestic situation[13]—and the neoclassic tragedy presented characters of significant social position. But in *The Fatal Extravagance* the major figures are former members of the gentry made destitute by the hero's gambling; in *Caelia* the heroine and her family are country gentry; in Lillo's *George Barnwell* a merchant's apprentice is the tragic hero; and in his *The Fatal Curiosity* (1736) the central characters are of an impoverished middle-class family. A principal aim of sentimental tragedy was to show the capacity for emotion and the "goodness of average human nature."[14] Sentimental comedy, however, generally presented characters of higher rank; but all sentimental drama was infused with a strong middle-class morality.

Also of interest are the character types that developed in sentimental comedy and their contrast to related types in the comedy of manners. The gay couple in the earlier type of play was now replaced by the man and woman of sense and feeling;[15] the attractive and gay libertine was exchanged for a more wicked nonsentimental figure, through whom vice was supposed to be made unattractive, but who generally underwent a remarkable metamorphosis and became a sentimental man of honor by the end of the play.[16] The grumpy old father, often trying to disinherit his son, gave place to the benevolent patriarch;[17] the crafty and humorous servant was transformed into the old and worthy family retainer;[18] and the bright, intriguing confidant became the sympathetic friend.[19] In many of the figures of the new sentimental comedy, morality and sentiment were the primary characteristics.

Sentimental drama, however, resulted not only from a reaction to the lack of morality in the drama but also, I believe, from a general humanitarian movement developing slowly throughout the eighteenth century, one that inspired such activities as prison reform and the founding of charitable societies.[20] The emphasis upon pity, benevolence, and the joys of altruism clearly links these plays with this movement. The statement of Bevil Junior, "If Pleasure be worth purchasing, how great a Pleasure is it to him, who has a true Taste of Life, to ease an Aking Heart. . . . This is the Effect of an humane Disposition, where there is only a general Tye of Nature, a common Necessity," expresses the humanitarianism of sentimental drama.

Though this new humanitarian sensibility was expressed and given an objective reality in the drama of the eighteenth century, it received its most developed statement in the works of Anthony Ashley Cooper, Third Earl of Shaftesbury, especially in his *An Inquiry Concerning Virtue and Merit,* which was published in 1699, three years after the production of *Love's Last Shift.* This treatise was later revised and included in a volume of his essays, *Characteristics* (1711), which had wide circulation throughout the eighteenth century. Shaftesbury claimed that mental pleasure and true virtue are to be achieved through "THE NATURAL AFFECTIONS (such as are found in Love, Complacency, Good-will, and in a Sympathy with the Kind of Species)."[21] *Characteristics* influenced philosophers such as Hutcheson and poets like Thomson and Akenside, all of whom furthered the cult of benevolence and feeling. Steele's *The Christian Hero* (1701) also manifests this new humanitarian sensibility—since "we lament with the Unfortunate, and rejoice with the Glad" we are "fram'd for mutual Kindness, good Will and Service"; and this humanitarian sensibility is evident in many of the *Tatler* and *Spectator* papers.[22]

When Richardson began to write his novels, the cult of sensibility had already found expression in the theater, in the writings of Shaftesbury and other philosophers, in poetry, and in the periodical essay. But it was the drama that most popularized this sensibility and most fully realized it as a creative force; and it was from the drama that Richardson clearly acquired many of the elements of his own sentimentalism.

The influence of sentimental drama on Richardson's novels is apparent. The very intention of his works is to evoke a sentimental reaction on the part of the reader who is to be improved by admiring, sympathizing, and even identifying with the novelist's noble characters, while condemning his immoral characters. Richardson's appeal to the reader's moral sensibility is at times crude and simple, but no earlier novelist had ever involved his reader so emotionally and morally in the lives of his characters. Nor had any previous writer of fiction been so flooded with letters of tender and righteous concern for the creatures of his imagination: "I entirely agree with her in every thing, sympathize in all her Distresses and Misfortunes, feel Pleasure or Pain only when Pamela does."[23] In his Postscript to *Clarissa* Richardson suggests part of his sentimental method: "He [Richardson] considered that the tragic poets have as seldom made their heroes true objects of pity, or the comic their laudable ones of imitation." Indeed, the novelist attempted to make his heroines both.

Pamela reveals the same emotional morality that characterizes t' ~ sentimental plays. But Richardson, in this particular novel, lie, ntly is more crude than many of his predecessors. The heroine's tears and platitudes are so abundant and often so indiscriminate that they distract from her power as a sympathetic character and from her credibility. Unnecessary cries of "I love my virtue!" and, as the following passage shows, an immoderate capacity for whining grief hardly commend to us her goodness or veracity: *"My dear Parents,* O let me take up my Complaint, and say, Never was poor Creature so unhappy, and so barbarously used as your *Pamela!* Indeed, my dear Father and Mother, my Heart's just broken! I can neither write as I should do, nor let it alone; for to whom but you can I vent my Griefs, and keep my poor Heart from bursting!" (I, 74). The degree of pity each character feels for Pamela often determines his or her moral stature in the novel: Mrs. Jervis is a good soul, for according to the heroine, she "could not help mingling Tears with my Tears" (I, 22); Mrs. Jewkes, on the other hand, is evil because she does not sympathize with Pamela; Mr. Longman, "poor, honest John," and Mr. Jonathan are virtuous because they pity Pamela; the servants in the country house are evil because they do not.

Clarissa also depicts an emotional struggle between virtue and vice. Belford, when discussing "What a fine Subject for Tragedy would the injuries of this Lady [Clarissa], and her behaviour under them make!" (VII, 132), says that from the heroine's conduct "a distress naturally arises, that must *worthily* affect every heart" (VII, 135). Once more the pathetic and undeserved suffering of an excellent woman is portrayed; once more Richardson calls upon his reader to feel the pleasures of pity and to be edified by the noble behavior of the distressed heroine. But the emotionalism in *Clarissa* is far more controlled than in *Pamela*. The first extended emotional passage does not appear until the eighth letter, in which Clarissa describes her initial battle with her parents over the odious Mr. Solmes:

> No expostulations! No *but's*, girl! No qualifyings!
> I will be obeyed, I tell you; and cheerfully too!—or
> you are no child of mine!
>   I wept.
>   Let me beseech you, my dear and ever-honoured
> Papa (and I dropt down on my knees), that I may have
> only your and my Mamma's will, and not my Brother's
> to obey.   (I, 53)

Following this episode the letters of Clarissa which fully describe her experiences manifest her extreme suffering, but to prevent prolonged emotionalism Richardson has his heroine present some relatively mild commentary and some description of action within such recounted scenes. The less emotional scenes described by Clarissa, her passages of pure exposition, the correspondence of Anna, and Lovelace's and Belford's early epistles suggest long intervals of equanimity. Later Lovelace describes the heroine's difficult trials before and after her rape, but the villain's letters are filled with reflective, cynical, and comic passages which preserve the emotional balance of the novel. After her rape Clarissa reveals her pathetic reactions and describes her past suffering. The heroine's repentance and self-willed death are then dramatically portrayed in Belford's letters. Although the heroine no longer suffers and seems remarkably calm, feeling runs high in those around her. But epistles from other characters keep in check the emotionalism of Belford's letters. Colonel Morden describes the long funeral scenes, which are shattered by Anna's horrible theatrical oration and descend into bathos when the four young virgins carry the coffin to church. After this event the novel regains something of its balance, and Lovelace's death is led up to and described in an emotionally controlled manner.

In *Clarissa,* as in *Pamela,* characters are morally divided according to emotional capability—those who feel deeply and pity the unfortunate contrast with those who lack such humanitarian sensibility. Belford's conversion to virtue results from his sympathy for Clarissa. Bella Harlowe is bad because she does not possess a "feeling heart." As Clarissa explains, her sister is deprived of the pleasure that emotions cause: "Bella has not a *feeling* heart. The highest joy in this life she is not capable of: But then she saves herself many griefs, by her impenetrableness—Yet, for ten times the pain that such a sensibility is attended with, would I not part with the pleasure it brings with it" (I, 320). Lovelace himself acknowledges his lack of a "feeling heart": "What's a tender heart good for!—Who can be happy that has a feeling heart?—And yet, thou'lt say, that he who has it not, must be a tyger, and no man" (V, 190). Lovelace almost admits that he is a villain because he cannot feel deeply. If he could feel deeply, he would pity Clarissa's suffering, convert to morality as a result, and marry his redeemer—such is the way of the sentimental world.

Only in presenting Harriet's struggle with Sir Hargrave and Clementina's internal conflict between love and religion does *Sir Charles Grandison* also treat the theme of virtue in distress. Otherwise the novel is generally concerned with characters who seem to exist merely to pity the difficult—though hardly distressing—situations of others and to feel pleasure in their own virtue and that of their acquaintances. Almost all the major figures of the work are models of morality, and, with the exception of Sir Charles, all are prepared to break forth in tears and platitudes at the slightest uneasiness of another person. Even more annoying is their capacity to cry when they encounter virtuous actions. They are pure figures of sensibility—men and women of feeling. As the sentimental dramatist had emphasized, it is noble to feel, and to show that one feels:

> Mercy! said Sir Rowland, in an accent that seemed between crying and laughing, You, you, you, madam, are a surprising Lady! I, I, I, never was so affected in my life. And he drew the back of his hand cross first one eye, then the other.
>
> O Sir Rowland, said I [Harriet], you are a good man. How affecting are the visible emotions of a manly heart! (*Sir Charles Grandison,* I, 136)

Although Sir Charles often seems incapable of experiencing deep feelings and displaying strong emotion, he continuously performs noble deeds that provoke reactions of strong sentiment in such characters as Harriet, Clementina, and Emily. Sir Charles admires the show of virtuous feelings in others. The radical nature of the sentimentalism and the general behavior of Sir Charles in the novel are well illustrated in the scene in which the hero finally proposes to Harriet. She can respond only with tears—much to the pleasure of the good man:

> Tears of joy strayed down my cheek, unperceived by me, till they fell upon his hand, as it had mine in it. He kissed them away. I was abashed . . .
>
> . . . . .
>
> Tears again strayed down my cheek. Why did I weep?
>
> Delicate sensibility! said he. He clasped his arms about me—But instantly withdrew them, as if recollecting himself—Pardon me, madam! (V, 185-86)

Present here are tears and joy—in the case of Harriet, tears from feeling joy; and in the case of Sir Charles, joy from her tears. But also present in the scene is the sentimental implication that both characters are highly moral because they can either feel deeply or at least appreciate such feelings in others.

The fact that emotions are displayed frequently and often without satisfactory cause is one of the reasons for the failure of *Sir Charles Grandison.* Though sentimentalism was in part a movement to portray the more normal feelings of people, its development both in the drama and in the novel led to these unnatural extremes of emotionalism. Richardson's success in *Clarissa* is largely dependent upon the cumulative power of the entire work. In such a totality, a balance between pathos and ethos is essential. Such proportion is absent in *Sir Charles Grandison*.

Like the sentimental playwrights in their advocacy of middle-class standards, Richardson treats with great respect the common domestic relationships. Part I of *Pamela* emphasizes the heroine's admirable behavior to her parents; part II describes Pamela's successful career as a wife and mother and is the first novel in English literature focused primarily on everyday family matters; *Clarissa* presents the relationship of parents and children as a major theme and chastises the heroine's family for its faulty conduct; and *Sir Charles Grandison* portrays in detail proper familial conduct.

In attempting to realize what was one of the main purposes of sentimental tragedy, the glorification of the virtues as well as the feelings of common humanity, Richardson chose characters from appropriate classes for his first two novels. Pamela is no higher in society than the merchant's apprentice, George Barnwell, in Lillo's play. In the main action of the first part of that novel only Mr. B. and Lady Davers belong to the upper class, and both manifest the immoral qualities of their social group. Considerable attention in the novel is given to Mr. B.'s servants and Pamela's poor parents. *Clarissa* is concerned largely with members of the wealthy middle class. Lovelace belongs to the nobility, but he is a symbol of the decadent and licentious element of his social group. In *Sir Charles Grandison* Richardson attempted to portray a model character for upper-class gentlemen, but created a hero quite middle-class in his opinions and attitudes.

In addition to basing many of his characters on types in the drama, the novelist also gave his figures the same qualities that the sentimental playwrights gave their men and women of feeling and their villains. Pamela and Clarissa have the same emotional and moral qualities as the females of sentimental drama who suffer for the sake of virtue; Mr. B. and Lovelace possess the same unfeeling hearts and immoral appetites as the nobles who attack middle-class values in such plays; Goodman Andrews, his wife, and the Sewards are given the same benevolent sensibilities as the typical parents and guardians in these dramas; and the elderly servants Mrs. Jervis, Mr. Jonathan, and Mrs. Norton are as faithful and full of tears as their sentimental dramatic counterparts.

The major figures in *Pamela* and *Sir Charles Grandison* may not satisfy the modern student of psychology, and certainly their emotionalism is frequently appalling, but the characters of all Richardson's novels were the most real and credible to appear in prose fiction. By bringing to his works the sentimental drama's stress upon the emotions, Richardson shifted the basic emphasis in the novel from action to human feeling and behavior. By using techniques adapted from the drama, the novelist was able to present fully such aspects of his characters: he had his major figures soliloquize about their own emotional states and thus allowed, for the first time in the novel, the developed portrayal of internal histories; he also had them describe dramatically their own emotional behaviors and that of other characters, and thus he created a world of more credible and realistic human beings.

The structure and pace of Richardson's novels differ considerably from those of earlier prose fiction partly because of this emphasis upon the emotions. Most novels before 1740 are episodic; they describe a large number of exciting adventures which are loosely linked. The pace of such works is fast because individual episodes are sketched briefly so that the reader may move on to other events of interest. But Richardson was more concerned with portraying his characters' feelings than with describing a succession of adventures. Few important events pass by without his heroines' carefully establishing their actions and states of mind; few scenes are described without their emotions being described in full. Richardson's novels, partly because of his emotional emphasis, are less episodic, more unified, and far closer to the pace of real life than any earlier work of prose fiction. His use of dramatic plots and rules and his graphic portrayal of scenes also affected these aspects of his works, but the writer's preoccupation with his major figure's feelings rather than with action and plot is a major factor in explaining why the pace and structure of his works differ so extensively from those of previous novels. A similar development had occurred in the theater. When sentimental drama is compared with other plays of the same and earlier periods, it is evident that the new emphasis on the emotions lessened the amount of action, as well as plot, and slowed the pace of the drama considerably.

Of Richardson's three novels, *Sir Charles Grandison* was most shaped in plot and structure by the author's sentimentalism. The novel generally is ignored today and with some justification: its hero is improbable and its action lethargic. But historically the work cannot be disregarded, since certain features in its plot and structure had a significant effect on later prose fiction. Such features can best be understood through an examination of certain Restoration and early eighteenth-century plays.

Two types of characterizations appeared frequently in the comedy of manners: the broadly drawn comic figure, who, in general, was motivated by a particular affectation or vice that the playwright satirized; and the hero and heroine, who, though often subtly drawn and possessing sufficient wit and colorful manners to make them quite attractive, also were controlled by an affectation or vice—but one generally not presented for ridicule and one sometimes tempered by the end of the play.[24] Etherege's *The Man of Mode; or, Sir Fopling Flutter* (1676) has such comic characters as Sir Fopling Flutter, whose ruling passion is for foppery, and Lady Woodvill, who is motivated primarily by a desire to live in the fashion of the past. The play's principal characters, although considerably more real and attractive than the comic humour figures, also are motivated by reigning passions—Dorimant for sexual alliances, and Harriet for coquetry. Similar characterizations appeared in other types of comedy of the period. Undoubtedly the plays of Ben

Jonson, both directly and indirectly, had some influence on such character portrayals.[25]

In the comedy of manners much dramatic action resulted from such portrayals in that each character's particular affectation or vice conflicted with that of one or more figures. For example, in Etherege's *The Man of Mode,* dramatic action results from the conflict between Dorimant's lust and Mrs. Loveit's jealousy, but their reigning passions also conflict with the humours of other characters, which are interacting among themselves. Bellinda's sexual pliancy, Harriet's coquetry, and Sir Fopling's foppery further complicate the action of the play.

The new type of figure that was developed in sentimental comedy was not ruled by affectation or vice. Instead, he was a virtuous person, concerned for the well-being and feelings of others. Only later, in such mildly satirical portraits as Goldsmith's Honeywood in *The Good Natur'd Man* (1768), did benevolence itself become a ruling passion and force its possessor to perform foolish acts. In general, the character of sensibility in comedy was a person of feeling, reason, good sense, and morality. Such sentimental comedies as Cibber's *The Careless Husband* portrayed both characters of humour and sensibility, with the interplay between both types responsible for the basic actions of the play. Lady Easy is virtuous, but her husband's promiscuity results in a dramatic conflict between them which leads to dramatic action. At the end of the play, however, Lady Easy's goodness converts her husband from his evil ways, and the dramatic action in which they are involved ends. Both characters have little more to do than utter virtuous sentiments in a static scene. In the subplot Lord Morelove behaves admirably, but has the misfortune to love Lady Betty Modish, who is motivated by vanity. Lady Betty's vanity is sufficient to bring her and her suitor into dramatic action.

The conclusion of the Lord and Lady Easy relationship in Cibber's *The Careless Husband* presented a problem that was to exist in entire plays which concentrated mostly on figures of sensibility. Among a group of people all motivated by virtue, there could not be strong personal conflicts; no characters of humour were present to provoke antagonisms and hence there was no significant dramatic action. This, then, was the logical extreme of sentimental literature—works in which action was minimized and hence plot deemphasized. In Steele's *The Conscious Lovers* and Hugh Kelly's *False Delicacy* (1768) there are neither major humour characters nor villains. The plots of these plays, mostly dependent upon misunderstandings and private conflicts between duty and personal desire, often seem uninteresting or contrived, and the real emphasis of these works is on sentiment and social manners.

Of Richardson's novels only *Sir Charles Grandison* shows the same type of plot and structure that developed in sentimental drama. Since the major characters are all people of sensibility, there is little action in the novel. No conflict exists between the hero and heroine because neither has an affectation or vice that could cause the slightest problem for the other. They are placed in the setting of Sir Charles' household, which itself is composed of a group of virtuous souls, incapable of exciting antagonism: Charlotte, though a gay lady, is still a woman of feeling; Emily is young and pure, and her innocent love for Sir Charles contributes only some pathos to the general situation; Lord G., Lord and Lady L., and Beauchamp also are characters of sensibility and do little more than talk virtuously. What develops among the principal characters is a series of unexciting conversations about personal matters, morality, decorum, and fashionable topics. Conflict, action, and plot are slight. Richardson's comic figures generally serve as contrasts to the hero and heroine and conversation pieces for the major characters; at most they function to induce Sir Charles and Harriet to acts of supreme benevolence. There is something sickly and appalling about the smugness and lack of vitality in *Sir Charles Grandison*. In the midst of the novel Richardson introduces Lady Clementina and her Italian family presumably to provoke action and develop plot. Though Sir Charles loves Harriet, he feels committed to marry Clementina; hence, like Bevil Junior, he is caught between the demands of his duty and his feelings. But Sir Charles is not a man to lose sight of his moral responsibility and so, with apparently little personal struggle, decides to marry the Italian woman, if she will have him. Clementina, however, is faced with a great dilemma and must choose between her religion and marriage to a man of another faith. Yet Richardson still gives much of his attention to the static Grandison household, and those scenes involving the Italian woman contrast sharply with the remainder of the work. Within Clementina, Richardson attempts to present a vital conflict possible in a world of non-villainous characters—a conflict between values that are correct, but incompatible.

Pamela is a sentimental comedy and *Clarissa* is a sentimental tragedy. In both works much of the action is motivated by nonsentimental figures. But *Sir Charles Grandison* is a sentimental drawing-room comedy; it has the same emphasis on morality and the emotions as Richardson's earlier works, but lacks the conflict that requires impulse from nonsentimental figures. Lacking significant action to relate, and incapable of a sustained presentation of Clementina's personal struggle, Richardson was forced to emphasize everyday relations and events as the basis of his characters' virtuous sentiments. Thus in *Sir Charles Grandison* great attention is given to ordinary social intercourse, to the manners and punctilio of characters, and to the minutiae of daily life. This is undoubtedly what impressed Jane Austen about the novel: "Every circumstance narrated in Sir Charles Grandison, all that was ever said or done in the cedar parlour, was familiar to her; and the wedding days of Lady L. and Lady G. were as well remembered as if they had been living friends."[26] Here was the first work of prose fiction containing a realistic drawing-room atmosphere and structured, for the most part, as a narration of everyday life in polite society.[27]

In *Sir Charles Grandison* significant conflict and a profound knowledge of human psychology are missing. Within static scenes the adherence to social manners, or abuse of them, evokes the display of human emotions, but unfortunately these emotions are more sentimental than real. But in so many ways *Sir Charles Grandison* made significant contributions in terms of subject matter, general emphasis, and structure. It begins the real domestic novel of manners and clearly points the way to the works of Jane Austen. By adapting elements from Richardson's work and from the eighteenth-century development of this type of novel, and by utilizing her own concepts of human behavior, dramatic conflict, and social commentary, Miss Austen was able to bring the novel to full maturity and create within it a truly complex and sophisticated comic world.

CHAPTER FOUR

The Tragedy
of Clarissa

Richardson generally thought of *Clarissa* as a tragedy, and he often defended the novel according to methods and rules of the tragic drama. In the "Prefatical Hints" Richardson claims that the work "is indeed intended to be of the Tragic Species";[1] in the Postscript to *Clarissa* he justifies his novel by the neoclassic concepts of poetic justice, the tragic hero, and unity of action, and he quotes at length from discussions of tragic theory by Addison and Rapin; and in the novel itself Richardson has Belford discuss Clarissa as a subject suitable for tragic presentation: "What a fine Subject for Tragedy would the injuries of this Lady, and her behaviour under them, both with regard to her implacable friends, and to her persecutor, make!" (VII, 132). But, Belford adds, since Clarissa's virtue was punished, her story lacks a moral proper for tragedy. Richardson expresses his disagreement with Belford in a footnote, in which he claims that the punishment of virtue is necessary for tragedy, and he defends the plot of his novel by the practice of tragic playwrights: "Mr. Belford's objection, That Virtue ought not to suffer in a Tragedy, is not well considered: Monimia in the Orphan, Belvidera in Venice Preserved, Athenias in Theodosius, Cordelia in Shakespeare's King Lear . . . are instances, that a Tragedy could hardly be justly called a Tragedy, if Virtue did not temporarily suffer, and Vice for a while triumph"[2] (VII, 132 *n*). Richardson frequently discusses *Clarissa* as a dramatic tragedy in his correspondence. To Aaron Hill he writes, "I intend more than a Novel or Romance by this Piece; and that it is of the Tragic Kind."[3] And in a letter to Lady Bradshaigh he claims that his novel evokes the necessary emotions of a "tragic performance": "Those Acts, Madam, may be called Acts of Horror by tender Spirits, which only ought to be called Acts of Terror and Warning. The Catastrophe of Shakespears Romeo and Juliet may be truly called *Horrid*. . . . I hope I have every where avoided, All Rant, Horror, . . . Terror and Fear and Pity are Essentials in a Tragic Performance."[4] All these quotations show that Richardson thought of *Clarissa* in the literary context of the tragic drama. What must be established now is the precise influence of this background on the novel itself.

That the dual purpose of tragedy is to teach and delight is a concept that appears frequently in the criticism of other periods, but never so often and with such insistence as in the criticism of the Restoration and early eighteenth century. Neoclassic critics took Aristotle's concept that tragedy was to evoke within the viewer's soul pity and fear and then purge him of these emotions and related it to Horace's "Aut prodesse aut delectare."[5] Dryden in his Preface to *Troilus and Cressida* (1679) explains the function of tragedy: "To instruct delightfully is the general end of all poetry. Philosophy instructs, but it performs its work by precept; which is not delightful, or not so delightful as example. To purge the passions by example, is therefore the particular instruction which belongs to Tragedy."[6] Dennis in *The Impartial Critick* (1693) claims that tragedy "removes the greatest Obstructions to Vertue, by reducing the Passions to a just mediocrity, from their violence and irregularity. And Secondly, because it teaches some Moral Doctrine by the Fable, which must always be allegorical and universal."[7] Charles Gildon in *The Complete Art of Poetry* (1718) also discusses the edifying powers of the emotions evoked by the drama: "Tragedy with an unfortunate Catastrophe is more delightful and more instructive; for, first it is more full of the Passions whose Motion causes Pleasure; and then it strikes us with the Punishment of the Hero."[8] Neoclassic critical theory, then, claimed that the spectator was taught by the obvious moral in the play and spiritually cleansed by the reduction of his passion. At the same time, he received edification and pleasure from experiencing the emotions displayed on the stage, as well as feeling pity and fear for the hero. Of course, other literary forms were supposed to edify and please. Comedy was to do both by ridiculing vice and folly. Early novelists frequently claimed that their works were edifying and entertaining. But tragedy was considered to be the literary form that best teaches and delights, and it was for tragedy that neoclassic critics established an elaborate body of rules that would assure this primary function.

Many dramas of the period influenced by neoclassic theory, however, seem little concerned with edifying the audience. Often in a concluding speech a character attempts to draw a moral lesson from the action: "Taught hence, Ye Parents, who from Nature stray, / And the great Ties of social Life betray; / Ne'er with your Children act a Tyrant's Part: / 'Tis yours to guide, not violate the Heart."[9] But the only improving function that most of these tragedies could have performed was to purge the spectator of the passions displayed on the stage; certainly their tragic protagonists were scarcely able to evoke pity and fear.

It was actually sentimental tragedy that best accomplished edification and pleasure. Hugh Blair's *Lectures on Rhetoric and Belles Lettres* shows that such a function was still part of the critical doctrine of the drama in 1783, but to be interpreted in sentimental terms: "Though innocent persons suffer, their suffering ought to be attended with such circumstances, as shall make virtue appear amiable and venerable; and shall render their condition, on the whole, preferable to that of bad men, who have prevailed against them."[10] Pleasure was to be achieved from sentimental tragedy not through the purging of passions but through virtuous sensibility.

It is likely that Richardson when writing *Clarissa* intended to satisfy those tragic functions advocated by the neoclassic critics but actually fulfilled by the sentimental tragedies. I do not claim that the novelist received his initial inspiration for the work from tragic theory or tragedy itself. He had already published *Pamela,* and now sought to write another of his "new species of writing."[11] Nor do I say that he received the idea for writing an edifying and entertaining work from the drama; indeed, much of the moral emphasis and didactic nature of *Clarissa* is traceable to his Puritan background, and it is the function of any literary genre to please. But once embarked on the work, Richardson apparently sought to satisfy the requirements of tragedy—"I intended more than a Novel or Romance by my Piece; and that it is of the Tragic Kind"[12]—and he worked out his characters and plot so that he might present his lesson in the tragic manner:

> Indeed, Madam, I could not think of leaving my Heroine short of Heaven: Nor that I should do well if I punished not so premeditated a Violation; and thereby made Pity on her Account, and Terror on his, join to complete my great End, for the sake of *Example* and *Warning.*[13]

> Clarissa . . . could not be rewarded in this World. To have given her her Reward here, as in a happy Marriage, would have been as if a Poet had placed his Catastrophe in the Third Act of his Play, when the Audience were *obliged* to expect two more. What greater moral Proof can be given of a World after this . . . than the Inequalities in the Distribution of Rewards and Punishments here below?[14]

Richardson attempted to write a tragic novel that would edify the reader through the death of the heroine and the punishment of the villain, and he developed his plot accordingly. But though he defended the actions of his novel on the basis that they evoke the tragic emotions within the reader demanded by neoclassic critics—"Terror and Fear and Pity are Essentials in a tragic Performance"[15]—he also made his role as a sentimental tragedian evident in his greater concern for pity than for terror: "He [Richardson himself] considered, that the Tragic poets have . . . seldom made their heroes true objects of pity."[16] The novelist even attempted to defend the sentimental moral-

ism of *Clarissa* on the basis of Greek tragedy: "Mr. Addison
. . . tells us, that Aristotle, in considering the Tragedies . . .
observes, that those which ended unhappily had always pleased
the people. . . . It cannot be supposed, that the Athenians, in
this their highest age of taste and politeness, were less humane,
less tender-hearted, than we of the present. But they were not
afraid of being moved, nor *ashamed* of shewing themselves to
be so, at the distresses they saw well painted and represented."[17]

Richardson belonged to a movement that made a more natural
and everyday humanity the subject of literature. This was
partly a result of his social background and a partly a result of
his revolt against earlier fiction—"They who read Romances and
Novels . . . when they take up Clarissa, not considering that
it is another kind of Work, or rather a new Species of Novel,
are apt to think it tedious, towards the Beginning especially,
because they have not the same Palate for natural Incidents,
as for imaginary Adventures; for the Workings of private and
domestic Passions, as for those of Kings, Heroes, Heroines; for
a story English as to its Scenes, Names, Manners, as for one that
is foreign."[18] In addition, he was influenced by the new sentimental tragedies which, though not many in number, were
successfully presenting more common figures. But though neoclassic tragedy presented high-ranking protagonists, the choice
of a middle-class heroine did not free Richardson from the
demands of the neoclassic doctrine concerning the principal
figure of tragedy.

Aristotle had said that the hero of tragedy ought to be a man
of less than perfect virtue: "The change of fortune presented
must not be the spectacle of a virtuous man brought from
prosperity to adversity. . . . Nor, again, should the downfall
of the utter villain be exhibited. . . . pity is aroused by the
unmerited fortune, fear by the misfortune of a man like ourselves. . . . There remains, then, the character between these
two extremes,—that of a man who is not eminently good and
just, yet whose misfortune is brought about not by vice or

depravity, but by some error or frailty."[19] Restoration and eighteenth-century critics agreed. Dennis in *The Impartial Critick* elaborates on Aristotle's concept of the tragic hero and defines him as "one who is neither vertuous in a sovereign degree, nor excessively vicious; but who keeping the middle between these extreams, is afflicted with some terrible calamity, for some involuntary fault."[20] In *An Essay on the Art, Rise, and Progress of the Stage* (1710), Gildon claims that tragic heroes "must not be either perfectly Virtuous and Innocent . . . nor scandalously wicked," but should be people who are good rather than bad, and who possess the common human "frailties."[21] Many heroes in different types of tragedy possess such "faults" or "frailties." In *Venice Preserv'd* Jaffeir, motivated by the desire for revenge, commits treason against a corrupt state and must die in spite of his noble qualities; the valiant Don Alonzo in *The Revenge* is destroyed by his own jealousy; in *Tancred and Sigismunda* Tancred's passion causes him to neglect his duty to his country and thus ultimately ruins him; and even Jane Shore, virtuous as she may appear during the play, in a moment of duress had succumbed to the immoral demands of the king and therefore is doomed.

Though most critics and many dramatists agreed that the hero should have a tragic flaw or human frailty, a number of heroes that appeared on the stage were perfect. Addison presented the hero of *Cato* as a flawless human being: virtuous and an example to all, he takes his own life rather than remain in a corrupt world. Dennis, however, criticized Addison for having selected a stoic as the hero of his tragedy—such a man has subdued his passions and keeps himself beyond the realm of human frailties.[22] Throughout the period virtue untarnished by human frailty frequently was represented by the heroines of the she-tragedy; when these ladies were not perfect their flaws were hidden beneath layers of virtue. The imperfect protagonists of sentimental tragedy also were characterized as extremely virtuous people in spite of their frailties.

Since Richardson considered his novel a work of "the Tragic Species," and since he viewed Clarissa as the heroine of a tragedy, his conception of her characterization was influenced by neoclassic theory and practice. The virtuous Clarissa is beset by a tragic flaw that brings about her downfall. But the heroine is portrayed as a virtuous character even when helping to cause her own destruction. Richardson was also influenced by the perfect or near-perfect heroines of the she-tragedy: Almeria in Congreve's *The Mourning Bride* (1697), Andromache in Philips' *The Distrest Mother,* and Mariamne in Fenton's play of the same name (1723) suffer undeservedly; and Monimia in Otway's *The Orphan* and Jane Shore, who possess human frailties, behave so admirably and achieve martyrdom in such a state of virtue that it is difficult to remember that they were not always perfect. The protagonists of sentimental tragedies, who received similar treatment, influenced Richardson in much the same way; for example, though George Barnwell murdered his uncle, he appears a saint before his execution, and though Beverley in Moore's *The Gamester* destroys himself through gambling, he is extremely virtuous in all other respects. Neoclassic tragedies, such as *Tancred and Sigismunda,* then, portrayed imperfect heroes who, being destroyed by major flaws, were supposed to cause the strong emotions of fear and pity in the audience, while the she-tragedy and sentimental tragedy presented central figures to evoke the softer emotions—figures who were excessively virtuous and whose noble characteristics were emphasized, even when they had erred previously. In his emphasis upon the saintly qualities and suffering of his heroine, Richardson depicted Clarissa very much as the protagonist of a she-tragedy and sentimental drama; at the same time, like many of the writers of these plays, he gave his central figure a neoclassic flaw in order to make her a tragic figure.

Richardson's attitude concerning Clarissa's responsibility for her tragic fate, however, was inconsistent. Like the dramatists he was following, he strongly emphasized his heroine's morality in the last part of his work, but one senses that Richardson by this time in his writing of the novel had completely convinced himself of Clarissa's perfection. In other parts of *Clarissa* as well, Richardson seems to present his heroine as spotless. The novelist at first wanted Clarissa to be both the heroine of a tragedy and a model for her sex—these two intentions were bound to conflict. It is this conflict which perhaps explains the reader's ambivalence toward Clarissa throughout the work: though Richardson intends her as a model of virtue, the heroine certainly does not seem wholly blameless for her misfortunes.[23]

Richardson wrote to Aaron Hill, "I had further intended to make her so faultless, that a Reader should find no way to account for the Calamities she met with."[24] But on other occasions he was willing to blame Clarissa, at least partly, for her misfortunes. On one of the pages in a copy of *Clarissa* that he sent to Lady Bradshaigh, Richardson stated, "I did not want [Clarissa] to be blameless."[25] In his Postscript to the novel Richardson defends his treatment of Clarissa by citing from *Spectator* 548 (Nov. 28, 1712) a passage that advocates the death of tragic heroes. The quoted critic, who is unknown, states, "The most perfect man has vices enough to draw down punishments upon his head, and to justify Providence in regard to any miseries that may befal him" (VIII, 312). At times the novelist made specific references to his heroine's improper behavior. Writing to Sarah Chapone, he said: "Clarissa might have been excused, if anybody. But I made her *appoint, repent,* and *resolve against* going off; Yet tricked away; and this, as a Consequence of her first Error, of Corresponding with Lovelace against Prohibition; tho' at first doing it on Motives not illaudable. Whence an important Moral results, To avoid the first Appearance of Evil."[26] In part of "Prefatical Hints," probably written by the Reverend Mr. Spence, a similar point is made about Clarissa's conduct:

> But this is the direct Moral of the whole Story: "That a Woman, even of the greatest Abilities, should not enter into any, even the most guarded, Correspondence with a Rake; and that if she once falls into his Power, she is undone."
>
> To enforce this Moral, it was necessary to Paint out all the Distresses of the Sufferer; and to make her suffer to the End.
>
> .   .   .   .   .
>
> Clarissa takes but one false Step in the whole Piece. She is impelled toward it, in general, by the strange

Behaviour of her Family; and betrayed into it, at the time, by the strange Contrivances of her Deceiver. But this single Step was of the utmost Consequence. It flings her into the Power of the most dangerous of men; and that makes all the Remainder of her Life melancholy and distressed.[27]

In much of the writing of *Clarissa* Richardson considered his heroine as partly to blame for her calamities because she willfully undertook a relationship with the rake, an act that, in spite of good intentions, was improper and dangerous.

But so much for Richardson's commentary. In examining the character of Clarissa and her behavior in a tragic world, we see that the heroine does err and that her calamities are brought about by a specific tragic flaw. Clarissa's mistake consists in befriending Lovelace despite the repeated warnings of both her family and friends; the result of her initial error is that she becomes vulnerable to his machinations. Clarissa is aware of Lovelace's evil qualities from the beginning:

> My Aunt Hervey, in confidence, gave me the following particulars of what the man said of him.
>
> .   .   .   .   .
>
> "He was a sad gentleman, he said, as to women:—If his tenants had pretty daughters, they chose to keep them out of his sight. . . . But for his Uncle's and Aunt's teazings, the man fancied he would not think of marriage: He was never known to be disguised with liquor; but was a great plotter, and a great writer: That he lived a wild life in town, . . . Had Six or Seven companions as bad as himself."   (I, 24)

Yet she corresponds with Lovelace, though she is forbidden to do so, and is made to realize the imprudence of this act:

> For altho' I was induced to carry on this unhappy correspondence, as I think I ought to call it, in hopes to prevent mischief; yet indiscreet measures are fallen upon by the rash man, before I, who am so much concerned in the event of the present contentions, can be

consulted: And between his violence on one hand, and that of my relations on the other, I find myself in danger from both.

O my dear! what is worldly wisdom but the height of folly?—I, the meanest, at least the youngest, of my Father's family, to thrust myself in the gap between such uncontroulable spirits! (II, 255)

Soon after, she writes Lovelace and makes an appointment with him to flee to his family; thus her initial error leads to another mistake in conduct. She is a virtuous woman and he an avowed libertine; the chemical equation is true to form and because of their meeting, Clarissa, though she has changed her mind, is tricked into leaving her home and then raped. After this crime is committed upon her she willingly submits to death because she blames herself for her fate. In a letter written after the sexual violation she recriminates herself in a parabolic manner:

A LADY took a great fancy to a young Lion, or a Bear, I forget which—But a Bear, or a Tyger, I believe, it was. It was made her a present of, when a whelp. She fed it with her own hand: She nursed up the wicked cub with great tenderness; and would play with it, without fear or apprehension of danger: And it was obedient to all her commands: And its tameness, as she used to boast, encreased with its growth; so that, like a Lapdog, it would follow her all over the house. But mind what followed: At last, some-how, neglecting to satisfy its hungry maw, or having otherwise disobliged it on some occasion, it resumed its nature; and on a sudden fell upon her, and tore her in pieces.—And who was most to blame, I pray? The Brute, or the Lady? The Lady, surely!—For what *she* did, was *out* of nature, *out* of character, at least: What *it* did, was *in* its own nature. (V, 329)

By eighteenth-century standards, Clarissa committed an error by submitting herself to a relationship with the libertine. What caused her to do so? What is the tragic flaw in her predominantly virtuous soul? Richardson is specific about her flaw: his heroine, shortly before her flight with Lovelace, rebukes herself for that enemy of tragic heroes, pride:

> I was the pride of all my friends, proud *myself* of *their* pride, and glorying in my standing. Who knows what the justice of Heaven may inflict, in order to convince us, that we are not out of the reach of misfortune; and to reduce us to a better reliance, than what we have hitherto presumptuously made?
>
> . . . *Strange,* I may well call it; for don't you see, my dear, that we seem all to be *impelled,* as it were, by a perverse fate, which none of us are able to resist?— And yet all arising (with a strong appearance of self-punishment) from ourselves? . . .
>
> . . . my calamities have humbled me enough to make me turn my gaudy eye inward; to make me look into myself.—And what have I discovered there?—Why, my dear friend, more *secret* pride and vanity than I could have thought had lain in my unexamined heart.
>
> (II, 263-64)

In this passage Clarissa acknowledges both her flaw and the tragic world in which she finds herself. Richardson is not ambiguous about the nature of his heroine's pride. Clarissa has an excessive faith in her own abilities, and it is this belief in her superiority which allows her to behave "presumptuously." In another passage she discusses her presumptuous behavior:

> O my dear! what is worldy wisdom but the height of folly?—I, the meanest, at least the youngest, of my Father's family, to thrust myself in the gap between such uncontroulable spirits!—To the intercepting perhaps of the designs of Providence, which may intend to make these hostile spirits their own punishers.— If so, what presumption!—Indeed, my dear friend, I am afraid I have thought myself of too much consequence. But, however this be, *it is good, when calamities befal us, that we should look into ourselves, and fear.* (II, 255)

The heroine's pride in her abilities results in a lack of caution and sufficient moral concern. Her pride causes her to form an improper relationship with the rake; it allows her to make plans to flee with him; and, once she is in Lovelace's power, Clarissa's pride evokes within her the belief that she can control a man who has not been controlled by any other woman. Later in the novel Clarissa discusses another "presumptuous" motive for having associated with Lovelace: "I had another motive, which I knew would of itself give me merit with your whole family; a presumptuous one (a punishably presumptuous one, as it proved) in the hope that I might be an humble means in the hand of Providence to reclaim a man, who had, as I thought, good sense enough at bottom to be reclaimed" (VI, 136-37). Clarissa had wished to reclaim a man for whom she felt affection, perhaps even love,[28] but whereas love conquered all in earlier fiction, it could not do so in Richardson's tragic novel.

In a similar manner Lovelace's characterization fulfills the neoclassic prescription for a tragic villain. Since Aristotle required that a hero be imperfect, neoclassic critics demanded that a villain possess some moral attributes and have some explanation for his evil deeds.[29] Dryden stated, "To produce a villain, without other reason than a natural inclination to villainy, is, in Poetry, to produce an effect without a cause; and to make him more a villain than he has just reason to be, is to make an effect which is stronger than the cause."[30] Rymer criticized Shakespeare for creating Iago as "a Rogue beyond what the Devil ever finish'd," and Dennis attacked Addison for the "too scandalous" characters of Sempronius and Syphax in *Cato*.[31] Tragedy was to give a moral lesson, and no value was to be received from the presentation of a completely wicked person. A villain who fulfills such neoclassic requirements is Zanga in Young's *The Revenge,* a play based upon Shakespeare's *Othello*. Don Alonzo formerly had beaten Zanga and killed his father; for these reasons Zanga encourages Alonzo's jealousy of his wife and provokes him to murder her. Before he receives his retribution on the rack, Zanga is moved by the virtue of his enemy. Lovelace also is not a complete villain:

"The Gentlemen, tho' professed Libertines . . . are not, however, either Infidels or Scoffers; nor yet such as think themselves freed from the observance of those other moral duties which bind man to man."[32] Lovelace is a fascinating combination of good and evil; his character has strong elements of nobility and dignity that make him one of Richardson's finest portrayals. Lovelace's motivation for ruining women is carefully established in the novel: having been hurt in a youthful love affair, he has sworn revenge on the female sex. His behavior to Clarissa also is a result of the insult he has received from her family. Like the heroine, he is strongly motivated by his pride, but in his case it becomes an obsession that drives him to criminal actions. That he becomes more evil as the novel progresses is chiefly a consequence of Richardson's reaction to the popularity that this character achieved among certain of his female readers. In his final scenes Lovelace once more is a morally complex creature.

The structure of *Clarissa* seems influenced by tragic theory and tragedy. A popular critical controversy of the time was concerned with the dramatic unities. Aristotle had required only the unity of action in a dramatic presentation: "The plot being an imitation of an action, must imitate one action and that a whole."[33] The neoclassic critics advocated unity of action. Thomas Rymer claimed that "an Author may multiply the *Incidents,* may add *Episods [sic],* and *thicken* the *Plot,* as he sees occasion; provided that all the *lines* tend to the same *center.*"[34] Addison stated that unity of action is necessary to prevent the dissipation of the audience's emotions, for in a play with a double plot, "though the Grief of the Audience, in such Performances, be not changed into another Passion, as in Tragi-Comedies; it is diverted upon another Object, which weakens their concern for the principal Action, and breaks the Tide of Sorrow, by throwing it into different Channels."[35] The neoclassic critics even praised Shakespeare for the single unity his works did possess: "There is not one Scene in the Play [*Hamlet*] but what some way or other conduces towards the Denoüement of the Whole; and thus the Unity of Action is indisputably kept up in every Thing tending to what we may call the main Design."[36] The dramatic action of a play was to be united by a major theme and organized into a single plot. This rule was followed in many of the tragedies of the period. Plays such as Southerne's *Oroonoko* (1695) were criticized for their double plots by critics like Addison.[37]

In his Postscript Richardson praises *Clarissa* in the critical terms of tragic theory for satisfying the unity of action: "A Story in which so many persons were concerned either principally or collaterally, and of characters and dispositions so various, carried on with tolerable connexion and perspicuity, in a series of Letters from different persons, without the aid of digressions and episodes foreign to the principal end and design, he [Richardson] thought had *novelty* to be pleaded for it" (VIII, 325).[38] Unity of action was not often present in earlier fiction; yet *Clarissa* is composed of eight volumes in which there are no digressive chapters or incidents.[39] Although Richardson's use of dramatic plots partly is responsible for this, I think it quite likely that he learned from tragedy and tragic theory to keep these plots unified.

Although Aristotle does not mention the unity of place, he observes that "Tragedy endeavors, as far as possible, to confine itself to a single revolution of the sun, or but slightly to exceed this limit."[40] The unities of time and place were much debated in neoclassic dramatic criticism until Johnson's attack on them seems to have sounded the death knell on the entire controversy. The playwrights themselves disagreed in practice: although many neoclassic tragedies possessed the unities of time and place, a large number did not. Wilbur L. Cross claims that *Clarissa's* duration of one year "is without doubt a conscious extension of the dramatist's one day to a fixed period more suitable to the novel."[41] A consideration of the time scheme of *Clarissa* in relation to that of the drama and fiction of the period suggests that Richardson followed the neoclassic rule of unity of time, but with some modification in order to satisfy the demands of a lengthy art form. The first letter of *Clarissa* is dated January 10 and the last, December 18 of the same year. The eight volumes of the work thus depict a series of events that occur in approximately one year.[42] Hence, the ratio of the time sequence of *Clarissa* to its length is proportionate to the ratio of the time sequence of a neoclassic tragedy to its length. The carefully specified duration of one year for the action of *Clarissa* appears particularly significant in relation to the vague or lengthy durations of action in earlier fiction. Some plots seem to have a timespan of less than a year, though one can rarely be certain, but in general the plots of most fiction before *Clarissa* have a timespan of anywhere from several years to the course of an entire life. That Richardson calls his work a history *(Clarissa; or, The History of a Young Lady)* indicates that he was influenced by preceding fiction—many earlier novels were called histories to make them seem authentic biographies, and a large number of these works presented the complete life of a character. That he imposes upon *Clarissa* a time restriction of one year seems to be another indication of the important influence of the tragic drama upon his novel.[43]

As installments of *Clarissa* were published Richardson was hounded by readers who advised him how to end the work and dispose of his major figures. Even after he had completed the novel he felt called upon to defend his conclusion, as is evident from his correspondence. Had his work been a tragedy for the stage, its length would have been five acts and the denouement would have quickly followed the major action of the play. But it was a novel, a very long novel, that was published in sections, thus permitting the public the luxury of living with the characters and sympathizing with them at leisure. Clarissa's demise was for the public like the death of an intimate friend. And even if read as an entirety, the work was long enough and the pace sufficiently slow to allow the reader the same type of intimacy with the characters.

Aristotle considered tragedies with happy endings inferior to those plays in which the hero dies, but the French classicists generally favored plays in which virtue was rewarded. Rymer also favored the latter type of tragedy and used the name "poetical justice" to describe the just distribution of rewards and punishments at the end of such a work.[44] Addison, however, was strongly opposed to tragedies that ended happily since "Good and Evil happen alike to all Men on this Side of the Grave; and as the principal Design of Tragedy is to raise Commiseration and Terror in the Minds of the Audience, we shall defeat this great End, if we always make Virtue and Innocence happy and successful."[45] Addison granted that a tragedy might present a happy ending and be successful, but he considered such a work as inferior to tragedy without poetic justice. Dennis disagreed with Addison, claiming that the moral function of drama made poetic justice necessary: "What Moral, where the Good and the Bad are confounded by Destiny, and perish alike promiscuously."[46] But Dennis stated that those plays which Aristotle had cited as ending unfortunately for the heroes actually satisfied poetic justice, since the protagonists were punished for flaws in their characters. He could have said the very same thing of those works which Addison cited as examples of plays without poetic justice. Aristotle, Dennis claimed, also had defended the concept of poetic justice by condemning the downfall of a perfect hero as the subject of tragedy. Earlier Dennis had presented a Christian defense of the death of a flawed tragic hero: "But then to make involuntary Faults capital, and to punish them with the last Punishment, would not be so consistent with the Goodness of God, unless there were a Compensation hereafter."[47] As for the drama of the period itself, such works as *The Mourning Bride, Alzira,* and *Irene* adhered to the rule of poetic justice, while a larger number of tragedies ended unhappily.[48]

Richardson in his Postscript to *Clarissa* uses established critical arguments both for and against poetic justice to defend the ending of his novel. He claims that "He was resolved . . . to attempt something that never yet had been done": "He [Richardson] considered, that the Tragic poets have as seldom made their heroes true objects of pity . . . : And still more rarely have made them in their deaths look forward to a *future hope.*"

He points out that the ending of his novel does in a way satisfy the requirements of "poetical justice": "After all, what is the Poetical Justice . . . but another sort of dispensation than that which God, by Revelation, teaches us, He has thought fit to exercise mankind; whom placing here only in a state of probation, he hath so intermingled good and evil, as to necessitate us to look forward for a more equal dispensation of both?" (VIII, 308-309). Richardson thus uses the only defense Dennis would allow for the death of a virtuous figure in tragedy—that such a death shows God's justice and goodness in the hereafter. The novelist then quotes almost all of Addison's argument against poetic justice in *Spectator* 40 to defend Clarissa's death. He also quotes *Spectator* 548 (Nov. 28, 1712) and Rapin's *Reflections on Aristotle's Treatise of Poesie* to justify his tragic ending. Richardson concludes his argument by claiming that "the notion of *poetical justice* founded on the *modern rules,* has hardly ever been more strictly observed in works of this nature than in the present performance," since Lovelace and other evil figures are punished, while Miss Howe, Mr. Hickman, Belford, and "the *worthy*" Mrs. Norton are rewarded.

That Richardson uses conflicting arguments from tragic theory to defend his novel does not negate the influence of such concepts on his work. It rather suggests that he tried to form an ending to *Clarissa* that would satisfy both the tragic nature of the novel and the principle of poetic justice. Because he was writing a work of "the Tragic Species," he felt the necessity for his heroine's death. But how would this accord with the moral function of his work? How would poetic justice be shown as existing not only in the world of *Clarissa,* but in the real world? Rymer's concept of poetic justice advocated the hero's triumph within the action of the play. Dennis' early interpretation of the principle allowed the death of a flawed protagonist, if it were shown that his virtues were rewarded in the hereafter. Rymer's concept was dramatically weak; Dennis' was not; and it is Dennis' concept that the novel follows. In the Postscript Richardson argues that his novel satisfies poetic justice through the promise of heavenly rewards for Clarissa, and then quotes *Spectator* 548, which defends the death of a hero on the basis that "The most perfect man has vices enough to draw down punishments upon his head."[49] Clarissa as a flawed character is destroyed, but her virtuous conduct is rewarded in the hereafter. Her triumph on earth could hardly present such a spectacular lesson in virtue and religion as her Christian death.

Although *Clarissa* complies with practices established in the contemporary drama and rules advocated by the tragic criticism of the time, Richardson also utilizes in his work basic dramatic techniques of the tragedians of all ages. John Reade wrote him that "There's a Cloud of Misfortune hangs over her first Appearance On the Stage, that attends her thro' every scene."[50] From the very beginning of the work the novelist carefully sustains an atmosphere of impending doom. Mrs. Norton's warning, Clarissa's foreboding letter on pride and the threatening disaster, her frantic note after her flight with Lovelace, her strange dream,[51] and Lovelace's letters to Belford never let us forget that we are involved in a tragic situation, and that the final calamities approach with relentless inevitability. The world of *Clarissa* is a tragic world and the fact that Richardson sustains such an impression for eight volumes is alone a sign of his tremendous creative strength.

Richardson uses a technique essential in tragedy, one that adds to this feeling of impending doom, when he dramatically increases tension before acts of violence. Clarissa's rape is foreshadowed once she is with Lovelace, but the inevitable event is constantly delayed. The reader watches her in the brothel, then in the home of Mrs. Moore, and again in the brothel. When the heroine again is captive in Mrs. Sinclair's house, Lovelace's intentions and power become more obvious. Belford writes several letters in which he urges the villain not to harm his captive. Richardson further delays the denouement by having Lovelace write a long letter in which he discusses his relationship with Clarissa, transcribes an entire epistle from his aunt, and describes a pathetic scene between the heroine and himself. The inevitable has been so delayed, the tension so heightened, that news of the actual event both shocks and relieves the reader. A similar technique is used to relate Lovelace's fatal duel. The inevitability of the event is established; it is only a matter of time before Lovelace must die. Several letters are recorded in which negotiations for the duel are described. Tension increases for many pages, but is finally released when Belford receives a letter from a hired servant which describes Lovelace's death.

Richardson's use of the servant to report the duel seems to have foundation in tragic theory and practice. The ancient Greek playwrights banished violence from the stage; such acts were described by strangers or servants. Addison and Gildon attacked the display of bloodshed in the eighteenth-century theater,[52] and in such neoclassic plays as Hill's *Athelwold* acts of violence were performed offstage but narrated by important characters. Since important figures were used to narrate violent actions in contemporary tragedy, Richardson's unusual use of the servant figure to narrate the duel may well have been suggested to him by the Greek drama with which he was familiar in translation. By using a servant to relate the duel, especially after the long dramatization of the heroine's death, Richardson presents Lovelace's death in a quiet but highly effective manner.

An impression of impending doom and the development of tension before acts of violence characterize most tragedies. They are evident in the tragedies of Shakespeare, with which Richardson had great familiarity, in neoclassic tragedies such as *Mariamne,* which held the stage during the author's own lifetime, and in *The London Merchant* and *The Fatal Curiosity,* the bourgeois tragedies of the contemporary playwright George Lillo, whom Richardson much esteemed. The novelist's use of these tragic elements leaves little doubt where he received his literary schooling.

The tragic view is a defined and limited one that carefully organizes and shapes dramatic material. But the novel is too much the art form of the middle class, too close to the world of everyday life, too large to be shaped easily by the tragic vision. It attempts to catch the pulse of life, the massive weight of human experience, the similarity of activity and emotions in all people. The basic pattern of the novel is generally not the pattern of tragedy; yet by consciously following the critical rules and dramas of his own period, Richardson created a tragic novel and embodied within eight volumes a tragic cosmos.

Clarissa is a tragic heroine who must perform two battles. One battle represents the universal struggle between good and evil. Clarissa is a symbol of goodness and virtue—she has erred because of pride and not because of inherent wickedness. Lovelace, in spite of his positive qualities, is the profligate nobleman, the useless in society, and hence the symbol of evil in the novel. Lovelace's central motive in the work is to violate Clarissa, a deed that will destroy her life and defy the moral code she exemplifies. Clarissa represents the best of middle-class morals, and Lovelace the basest qualities of the nobility.[53] But Clarissa must also battle her family. Here the nature of the struggle is more complex, for the Harlowes are not evil, and even possess some of the middle-class values that motivate the heroine. Indeed, Clarissa consistently wishes to be allied to her family. Her dilemma is that she cannot force her family to separate its moral values from its mercantile values.

Clarissa is a tragic heroine whose fate is consistently a matter of universal concern. She has "a quality of mind that somehow atones for the nature of the world in which . . . [she] *and* we live."[54] Though her pride causes her to err, she does not seem completely responsible for her destruction. Something more than pride is responsible for her suffering, as she herself realizes: "*Strange,* I may well call it; for don't you see, my dear, that we seem all to be *impelled,* as it were, by a perverse fate, which none of us are able to resist?—And yet all arising (with a strong appearance of self-punishment) from ourselves?" In most tragedies, external evil and circumstances place a noble human being in a position in which he is forced to perform such action that will prove disastrous for him. He then becomes powerless to prevent his change of fortune and downfall: "The 'necessity' of which we are now speaking must rather be of such a kind as to take its course even after the performance of all the 'free' actions that may be tried in an attempt at flight. When we see the catastrophe opposed by all free efforts of will and means, and can still trace its irruption as 'necessary'; when we can even trace, through the turmoil and anguish of this struggle to avert the catastrophe, a species of transcendent necessity: then and then only do we have an example before us of tragic 'necessity.' "[55] When the hero becomes conscious that his ruin is imminent, his character manifests a series of changes. First he undergoes a moral disintegration as he loses confidence in himself and in the justice in the world; then he wishes for death as an end to his suffering; and finally he achieves death, but only after having regained his spiritual strength through some understanding of the universe and a realization of the peace that awaits him in death.

Clarissa is a victim of her destiny, of the circumstances that have forced her to err. But she also is a victim of what Lucas calls tragic irony. Just as Oedipus commits the very act he tried to avoid, and Othello destroys the very woman upon whom his happiness depends,[56] so Clarissa brings about her own defilement. But although the story of Clarissa is a tragic statement of human blindness and the irony of fate, it also asserts the personal triumph and grandeur of its heroine.

CHAPTER FIVE

The Dramatic Novel

Extended narratives in prose had been written for centuries in England before Richardson began work on his novels. Like countless authors before him, he wrote his fiction by creating characters and involving them in a series of related actions, narrated through description and dialogue. He was not the first to call his novels histories, nor was he the first to use the epistolary form. But the differences between Richardson's novels and earlier fiction are significant; his works possess elements that rarely had appeared in fiction, elements that changed the entire concept of the novel. The very differences that distinguish Richardson's works from earlier fiction are those elements which are the basis of what we call the "modern novel."

Richardson's novels, using the character types and plot material of the drama, show the same interest in common humanity and its problems that was developing in the theater. The adventures of the hero in Mrs. Behn's *Oroonoko* (1688), the romantic courtship of Brown's Lindamira, and the story of the whore and thief Moll Flanders are at times depicted credibly, but African princes and thieves are not encountered in everyday life, and Lindamira is far too generalized to be part of the living world. When Mr. B. is not pursuing Pamela and Lovelace is not plotting against Clarissa, Richardson's stories are concerned with the conduct of a young servant girl, the relations between parents and children, and the problems of courtship. Richardson's novels also differ from earlier fiction in their portrayal of personality. In the romantic novels of Mrs. Behn and Mrs. Haywood there is little attempt at realistic characterization. Characters are used primarily to support the exciting events, and they are portrayed basically as romance types. In such novels of courtship and manners as *The Adventures of Lindamira* and Mrs. Davys' *The Reform'd Coquet,* there is a fuller but still limited portrayal of major figures: sometimes the heroes or heroines, based on dramatic types, suffer from some affectation or folly, but in most cases they are unindividualized, though contemporary, lovers. The secondary figures in this type of novel are often stock characters adapted from the drama. Though Defoe in his personal histories makes a greater attempt to depict realistically his major figures, they are considerably less developed than those in Richardson's novels. Both Moll and Roxana are seen in a number of situations, but they are not given consistent psychologically realistic characterizations and the variety of their internal states is limited. Modern critics, I believe, read more into Defoe's characters than either the author intended or the figures possess. Richardson analyzed more deeply the characters of the novel and displayed in them a larger number of mental and emotional states. He was able to accomplish this in large part by his skillful writing of letters in which the fictitious correspondent explicitly recreates his or her inward being.

But perhaps Richardson's most important achievement was his basic technique of narration. Most of the authors of earlier fiction narrated a multitude of events generally in a summary style. In *Moll Flanders,* when the heroine and her third husband arrive at an inn, the following scene takes place:

> I took the freedom one Day to tell him, that it was true I had receiv'd the Compliment of a Lover from him, namely, that he would take me without enquiring into my Fortune, and I would make him a suitable Return in this, *viz.* that I would make as little enquiry into his as consisted with Reason, but I hoped he would allow me to ask some Questions, which he should answer or not as he thought fit; one of these Questions related to our manner of Living, and the Place where, because I had heard he had a great Plan-

tation in *Virginia,* and I told him I did not care to be Transported.

He began from this Discourse to let me Voluntarily into all his Affairs, and to tell me in a frank open way, all his Circumstances, by which I found he was very well to pass in the World; but that great part of his Estate consisted of three Plantations, which he had in *Virginia,* which brought him in a very good Income of about 300*l.* a year; but that if he was to live upon them, would bring him in four times as much; very well, *thought* I, you shall carry me thither then as soon as you please, tho' I won't tell you so before hand.

I jested with him about the Figure he would make in *Virginia;* but found he would do any thing I desired, so I turn'd my Tale; I told him I had good Reason not to desire to go there to live, because if his Plantations were worth so much there, I had not a Fortune suitable to a Gentleman of 1200*l.* a Year, as he said his Estate would be.

He reply'd he did not ask what my Fortune was, he had told me from the beginning he would not, and he would be as good as his Word; but whatever it was, he assured me he would never desire me to go to *Virginia* with him, or go thither himself without me, unless I made it my Choice.   (I, 82)[1]

This scene, described in such a brief passage, is representative of many of the episodes in the entire work: there is no description of voice, gesture, movement, or action. The scene lacks vividness and drama. The reader is simply supplied by Moll with an indirect account of what she and her husband said. The author does not show the two characters talking together; he does not draw their appearances; he does not depict how they behave and what they do. Only occasionally does the novelist present a scene at any length, but then the emphasis most often is on unindividualized speech:

The old Lady said, I am afraid *Betty,* what I have said to you about my Son, has had some Influence upon you, and that you are Melancholy on his Account; Pray will you let me know how the Matter stands with you both? If it may not be improper, for as for *Robin*, he does nothing but Rally and Banter when I speak of it to him: Why truly madam, *said I*, that Matter stands as I wish it did not, and I shall be very Sincere with you in it, whatever befalls me. Mr. *Robert* has several times propos'd Marriage to me, which is what I had no Reason to expect, my poor Circumstances consider'd; but I have always resisted him, and that perhaps in Terms more possitive than became me, considering the Regard that I ought to have for every Branch of your Family. . . .

And is this possible, Mrs. *Betty*, says the Old Lady? *Then you have been much Juster to us than we have been to you; for we have all look'd upon you as a kind of a Snare to my Son. . . .*

As to the Truth of what I say, Madam, *said I*, I refer to your Son himself, if he will do me any Justice, he must tell you the Story just as I have told it.

(I, 48-49)

Defoe does not develop this scene to its full potential: nothing is graphic, visual, or alive about it. Neither is Moll's inner world portrayed dramatically. The illusion of reality is not created sufficiently on any level. A few times in the novel Defoe does give the reader a physical and spatial sense of a scene, but these are brief and never fully developed dramatic scenes:

The next thing of Moment, was an attempt at a Gentlewoman's gold Watch, it happen'd in a Crowd, at a Meeting-House, where I was in very great Danger of being taken; I had full hold of her Watch, but giving a great Jostle, as if somebody had thrust me against her, and in the Juncture giving the Watch a fair pull, I found it would not come, so I let it go that Moment, and cried as if I had been kill'd, that somebody had Trod upon my Foot, and that there was certainly *Pick-pockets* there; for some body or other had given a pull at my Watch, for you are to observe, that on these Adventures we always went very well Dress'd, and I had very good Cloths on, and a Gold Watch by my Side, as like a Lady as other Folks.

I had no sooner said so, but the other Gentlewoman cried out *a Pick-pocket* too, for some body, *she said,* had try'd to pull her Watch away.

When I touch'd her Watch, I was close to her, but when I cry'd out, I stop'd as it were short, and the Crowd bearing her forward a little, she made a Noise too, but it was at some Distance from me, so that she did not in the least suspect me, but when she cried out *a Pick-pocket,* some body cried out Ay, and here has been another, this Gentlewoman has been attempted too.

At that very instant, a little farther in the Crowd, and very Luckily too, they cried out *a Pick-pocket* again, and really seiz'd a young Fellow in the very Fact. This, tho' unhappy for the Wretch, was very opportunely for my Case, tho' I had carried it handsomely enough before, but now it was out of Doubt, and all the loose part of the Crowd ran that way, and the poor Boy was deliver'd up to the Rage of the Street.

(II, 26-27)

What is missing from so many of Defoe's scenes is a description of the characters reacting realistically to each statement and occurrence. He does give us circumstantial details in terms of clothing, loot, and the physical setting of a robbery, but the scenes in which they appear are never dramatized sufficiently. Nor, for that matter, is the narration ever given a dramatic dimension through the development of the point of view. Neither Moll's past nor her present inner states are presented with a sufficiently sustained reality to bring the individual episodes into a larger and more significant context.

Besides Defoe, the most skillful writers of fiction during the early decades of the eighteenth century were Mrs. Haywood and Mrs. Davys. Although the point of view of their novels is generally omnipotent, undramatic, and unintegrated, these writers do occasionally achieve a certain reality in their works through the presentation of a dramatic scene:

> I go (answered *Amena*) from a false Lover and a falser
> Friend: But why should I upbraid you (continu'd she,
> looking wildly sometimes on the Count, and sometimes
> on *Alovisa*) treacherous Pair? you know too well each
> other's Baseness, and my Wrongs. . . . As she spoke this,
> she struggled to get loose from *Alovisa's* Arms, who in
> Spite of the Amazement she was in, still held her.
> *D'Elmont* was no less confounded, and, intirely [*sic*]
> ignorant of the Meaning of what he heard, was at a
> loss how to reply, till she resumed her Reproaches in
> this Manner: Why, ye Monsters of Barbarity, said she,
> do you delight in beholding the Ruins you have made?[2]

The speech in this scene is highly artificial, but at least the
characters' words are presented directly, and some attention is
given to movement and expression. The novels of Mrs. Haywood and Mrs. Davys, however, are not focused upon such
scenes, but rather upon general descriptions of events and
relatively long episodes which are presented almost entirely
through unrealistic dialogue. Omitting physical as well as
psychological reality from most episodes and providing only
a few partially developed scenes, such authors had to find
many events to fill their books. Almost every work of early
fiction is characterized by the same structure. A large number
of episodes, many of them summarized, are strung together,
and the scenes that are presented in any length generally
depend almost solely upon dialogue. But Richardson developed
a different kind of scenic presentation:

> To be sure, Mr. Lovelace, if this matter be *ever to
> be,* it must be agreeable to me to have the full appro-
> bation of *one* side, since I cannot have that of the
> *other.*
>
> If this matter be ever to be! . . . Would to Heaven,
> my dearest life, added he, that, without complimenting
> *Any*-body, to-morrow might be the happiest day of my
> life!—What say you, my angel? With a trembling im-
> patience, that *seemed* not affected—What say you for
> to-morrow?
>
> It was likely, my dear, I could say much to it, or

name another day, had I been disposed to the latter, with such an *hinted delay from him.*

I was silent.

Next day, Madam, if not to-morrow?—

Had he given me *time,* to answer, it could not have been the affirmative, you must think—But *in the same breath* he went on—Or the *day after that?*—And taking both my hands in his, he stared me into a half-confusion—Would *you* have had patience with him, my dear?

No, no, said I, as calmly as possible, you cannot think that I should imagine there can be reason for such a hurry. It will be most agreeable, to be sure, for my Lord to be present.

I am all obedience and resignation, returned the wretch, with a self-pluming air, as if he had acquiesced to a proposal *made by me,* and had complimented me with a great piece of *self-denial.*

Is it not plain, my dear, that he designs to vex and teaze me? . . .

But when he would have *rewarded himself,* as he had heretofore called it, for this self-supposed concession, with a kiss, I repulsed him with a just and very sincere disdain.

He seemed both vexed and surprised, as one who had made the most agreeable proposals and concessions, and thought them ingratefully returned. He plainly said, that he thought our situation would entitle him to such an innocent freedom: And he was both amazed and grieved to be thus scornfully repulsed.

No reply could be made by me on such a subject. I abruptly broke from him. I recollect, as I passed by one of the pierglasses, that I saw in it his clenched hand offered in wrath to his forehead: The words, *Indifference, by his Soul, next to hatred,* I heard him speak: And something of *Ice* he mentioned: I heard not what. (IV, 110-12)

This passage evokes a number of reactions on the part of the reader: at first he is conscious of the surface action of the two people; then the significance of the entire episode changes for him as he recalls Lovelace's real intention, of which the heroine is ignorant; and finally the comments and general point of view of Clarissa, who is narrating the episode, further colors the meaning of the action for the reader. Throughout much of the novel Richardson thus portrays his heroine's blindness and thereby implies the differences between his figures' actions and their past, present, and future attitudes. In relation to this last point, although the novelist is quite insistent on giving the reader the impression that the action which the letter-writer describes is happening in the present, he is quite ready to use the time distinction between the occurrence and the narration of an event for dramatic purposes. But the success of his scene is dependent on other qualities. In the cited passage two characters are presented with a certain amount of psychological depth and complexity: Clarissa's fear and pride, as well as her present indignation over the past encounter, and Lovelace's dishonesty, lasciviousness, and pride during that former event are portrayed; at the same time we are made aware of the male-female psychological, social, and economic conflict that motivates them both to a large extent. The basic situation of the virgin and the rake was not new in literature, but the character types are presented in this novel with a unique reality.

A considerable part of Richardson's achievement in character portrayal in such passages as that quoted above is dependent upon his scenic achievement. Attitudes, movements, spatial relationships, qualities of voice are so specified that the reader envisions the entire scene exactly as it would have occurred in real life. It was Richardson who developed the dramatic, realistic, vivid, dimensional, and temporal scene and based much of his novels upon it. Hence, it was possible for him in *Pamela* and *Clarissa* to present the relatively limited but unified plots of the drama in novel form, for this narrative technique allowed him to concentrate on fewer episodes and emphasize character rather than action. Even though *Pamela II* and *Sir Charles Grandison* have little plot, they are far more unified and harmonious than most earlier novels because of the new emphasis upon the dramatic scene. But as well as dramatizing the individual scene, the novelist dramatizes the point of view through which the scene is observed. He develops the characterization of each narrator at great length, depicts in detail his or her present state of mind and previous emotional involvement in the recreated scenes, and thus brings to life all levels of action in the world of the novel.

It seems that Richardson and his admirers were somewhat aware of what he had accomplished in fiction. Note the following interesting passage which may have been written by the Reverend Mr. Spence in the "Prefatical Hints":

> The Writers of *Novels* and *Romances* have generally endeavoured to pick out the most pleasing Stories; to pass over the dry Parts in them; and to hurry the Reader on from one striking Event to another. Their *only* Aim seems to be that of making a Tissue of Adventures, which by their Strangeness and Variety are meant only to surprise and please. Nature they have not much in View; and Morality is often quite out of the Question with them.
>
> Instead of following this way of writing, the Author of Clarissa has attempted to give a plain and natural Account of an Affair that happened in a private Family, just in the manner that it did happen. He has aimed solely at following Nature; and giving the Sentiments of the Persons concerned, just as they flowed warm from their Hearts.[3]

Richardson's novels, according to this statement, differ from other contemporary fiction in their more natural story material and more natural and emotionally real characters; this passage also seems to hint at the novelist's more detailed scenes and more dramatic and integrated point of view. Richardson's methods of characterization and narration are the very techniques that revolutionized prose fiction and influenced the course of the future novel. Like his subject matter and character types, Richardson's methods of writing were influenced greatly by the drama; hence, they can best be understood in relation to the techniques of the playwright.

A performed drama is immediately real to our senses; it creates life before our eyes. We see the people and events, hear the voices and clamor of life. These same dramatic qualities are suggested by the playbook: dialogue and stage action are transcribed in words which suggest a pattern of images that create in our minds the entire scene.

It was this dimension that fiction required in order to create the illusion of a more normal world and treat life more seriously. Until 1740 the novel was a vehicle for improbable tales, semirealistic love affairs, and unusual personal histories. With its rudimentary narrative techniques the genre could relate no more. Its basic method of summarizing episodes and quickly narrating a multitude of adventures made its success dependent largely upon the excitement of events. Its techniques could not create real people; thus, it could hardly portray realistic situations and concern itself with important moral and social matters. What was required was a dramatic dimension that could create the inner lives and outward existences of human beings.

Richardson achieved this dimension by writing his novels to some extent as he would have written plays. In his Postscript to *Clarissa* he calls that work a "Dramatic Narrative" (VIII, 309), and he even placed at the beginning of *Clarissa* and *Sir Charles Grandison* the "Names *of the* Principal Persons" just as a playwright presents in the front of the publication of his work a list of characters. To understand Richardson's dramatic methods as a novelist, the three general techniques with which his characters write their letters must first be established. Frequently more than one of these techniques appear in the same letter, but each is used for different purposes.

In the Preface to *Clarissa* Richardson discusses the letters of that novel:

> All the Letters are written while the hearts of the writers must be supposed to be wholly engaged in their subjects (The events at the time generally dubious):

So that they abound not only with critical Situations, but with what may be called *instantaneous* Descriptions and Reflections (proper to be brought home to the breast of the youthful Reader); as also with affecting Conversations; many of them written in the dialogue or dramatic way.

"*Much more* lively and affecting, says one of the principal characters (Vol. VII. Let. 22.) must be the Style of those who write in the height of a *present* distress; the mind tortured by the pangs of uncertainty (the Events then hidden in the womb of Fate); *than* the dry, narrative, unanimated Style of a person relating difficulties and dangers surmounted, can be; the relater perfectly at ease; and if himself unmoved by his own Story, not likely greatly to affect the Reader."

(I, xiv)

Richardson is stating that his work is more realistic, moral, "affecting," and entertaining than previous novels because it recreates the immediate mental and emotional states of the characters and the immediate reality of individual episodes. When he speaks against those authors who write not "in the height of a *present* distress" but rather in "the dry, narrative, unanimated Style of a person relating difficulties and dangers surmounted," he attacks the very techniques of summary writing used by earlier novelists. But Richardson himself at times used such a narrative method. This technique occurs frequently in his earliest novel, *Pamela*:

In this Quandary, now considering, now crying, and not knowing what to do, I pass'd the Time in my Chamber till Evening; when desiring to be excus'd going to Supper, Mrs. *Jervis* came up to me, and said, Why must I sup without you Pamela? Come, I see you are troubled at something; tell me what is the Matter.

I begg'd I might be permitted to lie with her on Nights; for I was afraid of Spirits, and they would not hurt such a good Person as she. That was a silly Excuse, she said; for why was you not afraid of Spirits before?—(Indeed I did not think of that.) . . .

> She was so good to indulge me; but made haste to
> come up to-bed; and told the Servants, that I should
> lie with her, because she could not rest well, and would
> get me to read her to sleep; for she knew I lov'd
> Reading, she said.   (I, 21-22)

But even this episode is presented more skillfully than most
scenes in earlier fiction. Although it is significant to the plot
that *Pamela* begins to share the same bed as Mrs. Jervis, the
scene in which she asks permission of the woman to do so is
certainly not important dramatically. Hence, Richardson has
Pamela summarize hastily the scene in her epistle; but on two
occasions Mrs. Jervis breaks into a few lines of direct discourse
to give this briefly described episode a bit of dramatic reality.
Nevertheless, the scene is drawn quickly, and little attention
is given to speech and action.

In *Clarissa* there is less expository writing and the technique
becomes a device for quickly summarizing past events, linking
important actions, and preparing for an approaching scene.
Clarissa describes the visit of Dr. Lewis that precedes the
dramatized visit of her brother and sister:

> So the doctor came up.
> We had a conversation of near an hour before din-
> ner: But, to my surprize, he waved every-thing that
> would have led to the subject I supposed he wanted to
> talk about. At last, I asked him, If it were not thought
> strange I should be so long absent from church? He
> made me some handsome compliments upon it: But
> said, for his part, he had ever made it a rule to avoid
> interfering in the private concerns of families, unless
> desired to do so.
> I was prodigiously disappointed: But supposing that
> he was thought too just a man to be made a judge of in
> this cause, I led no more to it: Nor, when he was called
> down to dinner, did he take the least notice of leaving
> me behind him there.   (II, 183)

There is no attempt in this passage to depict a pathetic situation through Clarissa's voice and movements, nor is there an

attempt to develop character. Richardson merely wants to establish the fact that Clarissa's family has control of the pastor, and thus emphasize the hopelessness of her situation in the next scene. In *Sir Charles Grandison* Richardson uses "the dry style" of summary writing for similar purposes, but more sparingly.

Richardson's second technique of epistolary writing dramatizes the correspondent rather than action. In self-revealing passages the letter-writer's internal state is established and his or her personality further defined. Such passages are successful in creating character because they "are written while the hearts of the writers . . . [are] wholly engaged in their subjects." In many of these self-revealing sections the correspondent loses awareness of the recipient of the letter and seems to pour forth a dramatic soliloquy:

> Can violence enter into the heart of a wretch, who might entitle himself to all her willing, yet virtuous Love, and make the blessings he aspireth after, her *duty* to confer?—Begone, villain-purposes! Sink ye all to the hell that could only inspire ye! And I am then ready to throw myself at her feet, to confess my villainous designs, to avow my repentance, and to put it out of my power to act unworthily by such an excellence.
>
> How then comes it, that all these compassionate, and as some would call them, *honest* Sensibilities go off?—Why, Miss Howe will tell thee: She says, I am the *devil.*—By my conscience, I think he has at present a great share in me.   (IV, 239-40)

Lovelace here seems to step forward and deliver a monologue on his inner thoughts. Such soliloquies, functioning in Richardson's novels as they do in the theater, allow his characters to present their inner world with striking fullness. Long soliloquies were not uncommon in earlier fiction, but they were usually rhetorical, bloated, unreal, and frequently concerned with the passion of love. But Richardson's soliloquies are not set rhetorical pieces; they are dramatic, fairly realistic, and psychologically credible. The novelist's practice of having his characters disclose their thoughts and feelings in this manner indicates his ability to merge the theatrical soliloquy with the epistolary form, which is itself a natural vehicle for presenting states of mind.

But a more frequent type of the self-revealing passage is that in which the correspondent speaks more directly to another character while dramatically disclosing his or her thoughts and feelings:

> Her virtue, her resistance, which are her *merits,* are my *stimulatives.* Have I not told thee so twenty times over?
>
> *Devil,* as these girls between them call me, what of devil am I, but in my *Contrivances?* I am not more a devil than others, in the *End* I aim at; for when I have carried my point, it is still but *one* seduction. And I have perhaps been spared the guilt of *many* seductions in the time.
>
> What of uncommon would there be in this case, but for her watchfulness?—As well as I love intrigue and stratagem, dost think, that I had not rather have gained my end with less trouble and less guilt.
>
> (IV, 376)

Such letters by Lovelace are self-revealing in that he describes his immediate thoughts and feelings in a theatrical style that dramatizes his emotional state. Clarissa also exposes her inner world to her correspondent:

> Forgive, O forgive, my rambling. My peace is destroyed. My intellects are touched. And what flighty nonsense must you read, if now you will vouchsafe to correspond with me, as formerly!
>
> O my best, my dearest, my *only* friend! What a tale have I to unfold!—But still upon *Self,* this vile, this hated *Self!*—I will shake it off, if possible; and why should I not, since I think, except one wretch, I hate nothing so much? Self, then, be banished from *Self* one moment (for I doubt it *will* for no longer) to

> enquire after a *dearer* object, my beloved Anna Howe!
> —Whose mind, all robed in spotless white, charms and
> irradiates—But what would I say?—   (VI, 116)

This passage, written by Clarissa shortly after her rape, recreates the heroine's emotional existence in a manner not found in earlier prose fiction. By having the heroine write this letter so soon after her violation, Richardson reveals her immediate internal reactions to the experience. In the passage Clarissa's confusion melts into self-reproach, which then changes to self-disgust. She hesitates for a moment (in a parenthetical statement), then suddenly turns to the recipient of the letter, Anna Howe, for pity; but the thought of her virgin friend shocks her once more into a state of confusion and suffering. The vividness of these emotions is heightened by their being directed to another character. Throughout his novels Richardson has his major figures react to a variety of related experiences, until their complete emotional histories are revealed.

In a more playful manner than that of Clarissa, Harriet Byron in *Sir Charles Grandison* suggests her state of mind and personality by carrying on an imaginary dialogue with another character in her letter:

> Well, but will you not, my Harriet, methinks you
> ask, write with less openness, with more reserve, in
> apprehension of the rod which you know now hangs
> over your head?
> Indeed, I will not. . . .   (I, 95)

At times a series of brief related letters of this type by one or several characters gives an impression of continuous dialogue which is rarely received from earlier epistolary fiction. Certain topics are bandied back and forth, arguments are sustained, and questions are asked in one epistle and repeated and answered in the next. It is the disclosure of personal thoughts and feelings through a dramatic and sometimes talkative type of letter which distinguishes Richardson's second technique of writing and helps bring to the novel for the first time emotionally realistic and psychologically developed characters.

Richardson's third technique is in direct contrast to his self-revealing manner of writing, though it too furthers the reality and fullness of his characters. In earlier fiction the predominant technique is narrative summary. Novelists seldom present individual scenes at length, and when they do such episodes generally are based almost entirely upon dialogue. The domestic conduct books, such as Defoe's *The Family Instructor,* with which Richardson was familiar, also present scenes of pure dialogue. Only rarely, as sometimes in the novels of Mrs. Haywood and Mrs. Davys, do we get a more developed scene. But Richardson's novels present many fully described scenes that are obviously a result of his knowledge of the theater.[4] Clarissa, master of such a technique, partly describes for Anna Howe this method of narration: "And then you will always have me give you minute descriptions, nor suffer me to pass by the air and manner in which things are spoken that are to be taken notice of; rightly observing, that air and manner often express more than the accompanying words" (I, 8). An excellent example of this kind of writing appears early in *Clarissa* when the heroine describes a meeting between herself and her mother:

> Sit down when I bid you.
> I sat down.
> You look very sullen, Clary.
> I hope not, Madam.
> If children would always be children—parents—And there she stopt.
> She then went to her toilette, and looked in the glass, and gave half a sigh—The other half, as if she would not have sighed could she have helped it, she gently hem'd away.
> I don't love to see the girl look so sullen.
> Indeed, Madam, I am not sullen.—And I arose, and, turning from her, drew out my handkerchief; for the tears ran down my cheeks.
> I thought, by the glass before me, I saw the *Mother* in her softened eye cast towards me. But her words confirmed not the hoped-for tenderness.

One of the most provoking things in the world is, to have people cry for what they can help!

I wish to heaven I could, Madam!—And I sobbed again.

.   .   .   .   .

I could hold no longer; but threw myself at her feet: O my dearest Mamma! Let me know all I am to suffer: Let me know what I am to be!—I *will* bear it, if I *can* bear it: but your displeasure I cannot bear!

Leave me, leave me, Clary Harlowe!—No kneeling! —Limbs so supple; Will so stubborn!—Rise, I tell you.

I cannot rise! I will disobey my Mamma, when she bids me leave her without being reconciled to me! No sullens, my Mamma: No perverseness: But worse than either: This is direct disobedience!—Yet tear not yourself from me [wrapping my arms about her as I kneeled; she struggling to get from me; my face lifted up to hers, with eyes running over, that spoke not my heart if they were not all humility and reverence] You must not, must not, tear yourself from me! [for still the dear Lady struggled, and looked this way and that, in a sweet disorder, as if she knew not what to do].—I will neither rise, nor leave you, nor let you go, till you say you are not angry with me.

O thou ever-moving child of my heart! [folding her dear arms about my neck, as mine embraced her knees] Why was this talk—But leave me!—You have discomposed me beyond expression! Leave me my dear!—I won't be angry with you—if I can help it—if you'll be good.

I arose trembling, and hardly knowing what I did, or how I stood or walked, withdrew to my chamber.

(I, 130-32)

Dialogue is presented directly; speech is individualized; movement and behavior are documented. The time duration of reading the passage approximates the duration of the event itself, since we are given a complete transcription of what was said and done. The scene is more minute, dimensional, temporal, visual, and real than any in previous prose fiction.

Presented is a world in depth within which speech and action occur second by second. The relationship between the mother and daughter is carefully defined and their personalities are made evident by choice of words, specified qualities of voice, description of action, gesture, and facial expression. Richardson has given a dramatic dimension to the episode by imagining it as if it occurred on a stage and by blending the formal elements of the playscript with the narrative mode of writing. The method of this passage is sufficiently dependent upon the formal techniques of a dramatic script so that by impersonalizing the first person statements, rearranging the spacing, and altering only a few sentences, we can obtain an actual play form:

> *Mrs. Harlowe.* Sit down when I bid you. [Clarissa sits down.] You look very sullen, Clary.
> *Clarissa.* I hope not, Madam.
> *Mrs. Harlowe.* If children would always be children—parents—[She goes to her toilette, looks in the glass, and gives a half sigh.] I don't love to see the girl look so sullen.
> *Clarissa.* Indeed, Madam, I am not sullen. [Rises and turning from Mrs. Harlowe, draws out her hankerchief.]
> *Mrs. Harlowe.* [Looking softly at Clarissa in the glass, but speaking not tenderly.] One of the most provoking things in the world is, to have people cry for what they can help!
> *Clarissa.* I wish to heaven I could, Madam! [Sobs.]

It is important to realize that the novelist generally describes more stage action in these scenes than would a playwright in an eighteenth-century playbook. A drama was written to be performed in the theater, and the playwright depended upon the actors themselves to supply much of the stage business. Richardson's medium was solely the printed word, and it was necessary for him to describe entirely an individual scene as it would appear on the stage. But in his dramatic scenes the novelist, as if he were a playwright, emphasizes dialogue more than any other factor. Such conversations, presented in the pseudorealistic speech of contemporary drama, are far more real than those in earlier fiction. Richardson's dialogue at least is individualized and has the language, sentence structure, rhythm, and tone of articulated speech.

Frequently Richardson's dependence on play form is more obvious than in the previously quoted scene:

> Shall I conduct your Ladyship down? [offering to take my declined hand.]
> What! not vouchsafe to answer me?
> I turned from her in silence.
> What! turn your back upon me too!—Shall I bring your Mamma to you, Love? [following me, and taking my struggling hand] What! not speak yet! Come, my sullen, silent dear, speak one word to me—You must say *two* very soon to Mr. Solmes, I can tell you that.
> Then [gushing out into tears, which I could not hold in longer] they shall be the last words I will ever speak.   (I, 330)

Here the paragraphing, the separation into brackets of the description of action, and the use of the present participle to describe that action, clearly indicate the influence of the dramatic script. Only a few alterations are needed to change the passage into actual play form:

> *Bella.* Shall I conduct your Ladyship down [offering to take Clarissa's declining hand.] What! not vouchsafe to answer me? [Clarissa turns from her in silence.] What! turn your back upon me too!—Shall I bring up your Mamma to you, Love? [following Clarissa, and taking her struggling hand.] What! not speak yet! Come, my sullen, silent dear, speak one word to me—You must say *two* very soon to Mr. Solmes, I can tell you that.
> *Clarissa.* [gushing out into tears.] Then they shall be the last words I will ever speak.

In the letters of Anna and Lovelace in *Clarissa* Richardson frequently uses play form, but with more details of action:

113

> *M.* [Lips drawn closer; Eye raised] Why, my
> dear!—I cannot but own—But how, I wonder, could
> you think of Mr. Antony Harlowe?
> *D.* How, Madam, could I think of any-body else?
> *M.* How could you think of any-body *else!*—
> [angrily, and drawing back her face] But do you know
> the subject, Nancy? (IV, 172-73)

Clarissa often writes in a dramatic style, but she never uses
exact play form. In *Sir Charles Grandison* scenes frequently
appear in play form. Harriet Byron often describes total scenes
in such a manner:

> *Sir Ch.* I have a Letter of his to answer. He is
> very urgent with me for my interest with you. I am to
> answer it. Will you tell me, my sister (giving her the
> Letter) what I shall say?
> *Miss Gr.* [*after perusing it*] Why, ay, poor man!
> he is very much in love. (II, 408)

At times names are omitted before speeches, but the form of
the dramatic script is still evident. Harriet does not use the
play form or near-play form if she was involved emotionally
in the scene when it took place and not a passive spectator,
but her descriptions still maintain the characteristics of the
dramatic style of writing in their full presentation of dialogue
and movement:

> He then on one knee, taking my passive hand
> between both his, and kissing it, once, twice, thrice—
> Repeat, dear, and ever-dear, Miss Byron, that this is
> *all* your doubt [I bowed assentingly: I could not
> speak.]—A happy, an easy task is mine! . . .
> I took out my handkerchief—My dear **Miss Byron,**
> proceeded he. (V, 145)

Richardson's correspondents rarely use exact play form to
describe events in which they were seriously involved. Each
correspondent's past involvement and often present attitude
evoke a complex point of view that colors the action and
prevents the complete objectivity of a playscript. Although

the event is portrayed dramatically and the narrator presents himself or herself as one of the figures in the scene, the reader is made aware of the narrator's past and frequently his or her present reactions to the event that occurred. Passages written by Lovelace often appear as pages from a playbook since he relates events which, though of tragic consequence to Clarissa, present no threat to his own well-being. But Lovelace's use of this technique also manifests the mocking manner in which he views himself and Clarissa as part of a drama. Only when the heroine is near dying is Lovelace shocked into reality; he then relinquishes play form.

Richardson developed the dramatic dimension in his episodes more and more throughout his three novels. In his first novel, *Pamela,* the heroine's personality and point of view receive more dramatic emphasis than the individual scenes. Though much of the work is composed of brief episodes of dialogue and passages of exposition, Pamela constantly interposes her own thoughts and feelings. But the fact that so much of the work is in the form of brief scenes of dialogue and that some of these scenes do achieve a certain dramatic quality is significant:

> Here was *John,* as I said; and the poor Man came to me, with Mrs. *Jewkes,* who whisper'd that I would say nothing about the Shoes, for my *own* sake, as she said. The poor Man saw my Distress, by my red Eyes, and my haggard Looks, I suppose; for I have had a sad Time of it, you must needs think; and tho' he would have hid it, if he could, yet his own Eyes ran over. Oh, Mrs. *Pamela!* said he; Oh Mrs. *Pamela!*—Well, honest Fellow-servant, said I, I cannot help it at present. (I, 152)

The scene begins hastily with Pamela's bringing in John and Mrs. Jervis and relating indirectly the woman's warning; but before beginning a direct account of her conversation with John, the heroine interjects, as a result of the man's reaction, a brief description of her own appearance. In *Pamela II,* when the heroine is not lecturing, there is an increased emphasis on individual scenes, which seem closer to dramatic form:

Are you angry, Widow?

She affected a Laugh: No indeed; it i'n't worth
while.

He turn'd to me—and I was afraid of some such
Hit as he gave me—I hope, Friend, thou art prepared
with a Father for the Light within thee?—That was his
free Word.

Is this Wit? said I, turning to Miss: I have enough
of this Diversion, where nothing but coarse Jests
appear *barefac'd*.   (IV, 96)

Here all the dialogue is related directly, and each character's
movement is described; as a result the time of the scene is not
foreshortened, and a full, dramatized account of what took
place is presented.

The Preface to *Clarissa* and the heroine's discussion of her
writing style show that Richardson in his second novel is
attempting consciously to make many of the episodes of his
work more visible and real. Richardson visualizes his episodes
as if they took place on a stage. This is obvious in a few of
the more theatrical scenes:

And into a den they led me, with broken walls, which
had been papered, as I saw by a multitude of tacks,
and some torn bits held on by the rusty heads.

.   .   .   .   .

A bed at one corner, with coarse curtains tacked up
at the feet to the ceiling. . . .

The windows dark and double-barred, the tops
boarded up to save mending. . . .

.   .   .   .   .

She was kneeling in a corner of the room, near the
dismal window, against the table, on an old bolster
(as it seemed to be) of the cane couch, half-covered
with her handkerchief; her back to the door; which
was only shut to [No need of fastenings!]; her arms
crossed upon the table, the fore-finger of her right-
hand in her bible. She had perhaps been reading in it,
and could read no longer. Paper, pens, ink, lay by her

book on the table. Her dress was white damask,
exceedingly neat; but her stays seemed not tight-laced.
. . . Her headdress was a little discomposed; her charming hair, in natural ringlets, as you have heretofore
described it, but a little tangled, as if not lately comb'd,
irregularly shading one side of the loveliest neck in
the world; as her disordered, rumpled handkerchief
did the other. Her face . . . was reclined, when we
entered, upon her crossed arms; but so, as not more
than one side of it to be hid.   (VI, 297-98)

Here the detailed description of setting (something uncommon
in earlier fiction) and of the heroine in a melodramatic pose
gives a suspended, stagelike effect. This highly theatrical
composition of setting and character seems to be taken directly
from the stage or from an illustration in a playbook.[5]

But more important are the natural dramatic elements that
the novelist emphasizes in his scenes:

> He took the removed chair, and drew it so near
> mine, squatting in it with his ugly weight, that he
> pressed upon my hoop.—I was so offended (all I had
> heard, as I said, in my head) that I removed to another
> chair. I own I had too little command of myself. It
> gave my Brother and Sister too much advantage. I
> dare say they took it. But I did it involuntarily, I
> think. I could not help it.—I knew not what I did.
> I saw that my Father was excessively displeased.
> When angry, no man's countenance ever shews it so
> much as my Father's. Clarissa Harlowe! said he with a
> big voice—and there he stopped.—Sir! said I, trembling
> and curtsying (for I *had* not then sat down again):
> And put my chair nearer the wretch, and sat down—My
> face, as I could feel, all in a glow.
> Make Tea, child, said my kind Mamma: Sit by me,
> Love; and make Tea.   (I, 100)

There is here a remarkable sense of realistic characters speaking
and moving in a spatial and temporal world. But though Clarissa makes a conscious attempt to recreate the scene dramatically and precisely, she is more than a passive spectator. The

awkward movements of Mr. Solmes, her own defensive actions, Mr. Harlowe's facial expressions and the tone of his harsh voice, and the conversation are all woven carefully into a pattern with Clarissa's observations and thoughts.

Lovelace at times shows remarkable skill in adapting the dramatic style of writing to his own evil and energetic personality:

> What's the matter, Dorcas?
>
> Nothing, Madam.
>
> My Beloved wonders she has not seen me this morning, no doubt; but is too shy to say she wonders. Repeated What's the matter, however, as Dorcas runs up and down stairs by her door, bring on, Oh! Madam, my master! my poor master!
>
> What! How! When!—And all the monosyllables of surprise.
>
> [*Within parenthesis* let me tell thee, that I have often thought, that the little words in the Republic of Letters, like the little folks in a nation, are the most significant. . . .]
>
> I must not tell you, Madam—My master ordered me not to tell you—But he is in a worse way than he thinks for!—But he would not have *you* frighted.
>
> High concern took possession of every sweet feature. She pitied me!—By my soul, she pitied me!
>
> Where is he?
>
> Too much in a hurry for good-manners [*Another parenthesis, Jack!* Good-manners are so little natural. . . .] I cannot stay to answer questions, cries the wench —tho' desirous to answer [*A third parenthesis*—Like the people crying proclamations. . . .] This hurry puts the Lady in a hurry to ask [*A fourth,* by way of embellishing the third!] . . .
>
> At last, O Lord! let Mrs. Lovelace know!—There is danger to be sure! whisper from one Nymph to another; but at the door, and so loud, that my listening Fair-one might hear.
>
> Out she darts—As how! as how, Dorcas!
>
> O Madam—A vomiting of blood! A vessel broke, to be sure.

> Down she hastens; finds every one as busy over my
> blood in the entry, as if it were that of the Neopolitan
> saint.
>
> In steps my Charmer, with a face of sweet concern.
> *How do you,* Mr. Lovelace?   (IV, 292-94)

In this passage Lovelace uses the present tense and supplies
a number of sudden exclamations to give immediacy to the
episode and to intensify the rush and chaos of the action.
He also uses long parenthetical statements to break suddenly
the movement of the scene and impose grotesquely upon it
his mockery and superiority. In such epistles Richardson seems
to achieve the very height of his narrative skills, for here the
dramatized point of view is integrated fully with the dramatized
scene.

Richardson developed his dramatic technique to an extreme
in *Sir Charles Grandison,* and the novel somewhat resembles
a long dramatic script. Many scenes are in play form. Other
scenes in narrative form give such little attention to point of
view and action and so much attention to dialogue that they
strongly suggest play form. Page after page is devoted to
dialogue, and it often seems that the characters have not moved
for a long duration. I suggested earlier that the excessively
sentimental and benevolent nature of the novel's characters is
the cause for a lack of conflict and dramatic action. The use,
therefore, of long scenes composed mostly of carefully recorded
conversations emphasizes the plotless nature of the work and
adds to its static quality. But the episodes concerning Lady
Clementina contain conflict and action, and Richardson dramatizes her scenes by describing dialogue, movement, gesture, and
expression. The dramatic dimension could be achieved in the
novel form only when the characters' situations were themselves
inherently dramatic.

Richardson's use of the basic elements of the playbook to
various degrees and with certain modifications is largely responsible for the dramatic dimension in his novels. But it is those

scenes, as the one between Clarissa and her mother quoted earlier,[6] in which the novelist blends harmoniously the form of the dramatic script with that of traditional narration that he makes a significant contribution to the art of the novel, for here he employs one of the basic techniques of future novelists, the narrative-dramatic style of writing, which describes and creates the scene while keeping it within the narrative rhythm of the entire work. The form of such scenes is not sufficiently different from that of regular narration to disturb us. Dialogue and stage actions fit into a pattern of narrative exposition, and speech, movement, and emotional reactions are described by a single narrative voice, maintained consistently throughout the work or throughout large sections of the work. It seems that John Reade was aware of this achievement when he wrote to the novelist, "It must be own'd that you have with uncommon Dexterity intermix'd the Narrative with the Drama without once losing sight of the Actors."[7] Novelists after Richardson used this technique to different extents; the degree of the dramatization of their scenes depended upon the total intention and structure of their works. Fielding was neither a psychologist nor a sentimentalist, and so he avoided giving the reader a closeup presentation of his characters. At the same time, the narrative viewpoint he emphasized continuously was his own, the writer's omnipotent perspective; hence, there is always a sense of his detachment in the presentation of episodes, and the scenes are never fully dramatized. But Fielding developed his *Joseph Andrews, Tom Jones,* and *Amelia* along the lines that Richardson had established: a single plot involving a group of major figures is developed through the presentation of a series of related episodes which are basically dramatic. The narrative-dramatic technique had become so established by the time of *Tristram Shandy* that Sterne played jester with it and presented his scenes with an exaggerated emphasis upon movement, gesture, and attitude. He also wrote these episodes so that their durations seem as long as the durations of such events in the minds of his characters. Sterne constructed his work as a series of related scenes, each presented in an absurdly dramatic manner, but instead of connecting his episodes by the chronological movement of plot, he connected them by their relationships in Tristram's mind. The narrative-dramatic episode, presented with moderation and properly integrated with point of view, was to become the basis of fiction for the next two hundred years. Jane Austen used it with skill and taste: embedded within her own ironic commentary and the point of view of her heroines, it was the very means by which she made real the world in which her leading characters found themselves. Dickens failed in his treatment of narrative voice and point of view, but he created a grotesque realism never achieved before in the novel through his superb use of the narrative-dramatic episode. Thackeray, like Fielding, moderately dramatized his episodes, but he used them as momentary flashes, glimpses into reality that suddenly illustrate and extend his own commentary. George Eliot used point of view masterfully in *Middlemarch* to shift focus among a societal panorama, the narrative-dramatic scene, and the consciousness of her characters. Finally, the works of Henry James constitute a significant development from the novel as a series of distinct but related narrative-dramatic scenes to the novel presented largely through the fluid consciousness of character. Though his early fiction is basically scenic, in his final works the scenes are deemphasized considerably and function mainly to set off reflections and currents of thought in the dramatized point of view. James Joyce's *Ulysses* and Virginia Woolf's *Mrs. Dalloway* and *To The Lighthouse* operate in much the same way, though they portray different levels of consciousness. After such works by these last three writers, the important English novelists became more traditional and based their works largely on the narrative-dramatic scene.

The English novel after 1740 might well be called the "dramatic novel," since beginning with the works of Richardson it differs from preceding fiction in its dramatic presentation of character and situation. Edwin Muir, however, in *The Structure of the Novel* uses the term "dramatic novel" to describe a particular type of modern fiction: "The plot of the dramatic novel [is] intensive. . . . The action . . . begins never with a single figure, but with two or more; it starts from several points on its circumference, which is a complex, not a nucleus, of personal relationships, and works towards the centre, towards one action in which all the subsidiary actions are gathered up and resolved. . . . The dramatic novel, while not altering its setting, shows us the complete human range of experience in the actors themselves. . . . Here the scene is changeless, and the characters change by their interaction on one another."[8] The group of modern novels that Muir describes is of interest to this study because Richardson, I believe, was the first author to write such fiction and is probably responsible for its development. The "intensive" plot, the events that begin with several figures and work "towards one action in which all the subsidiary actions are gathered up and resolved," the "changeless" scene and changing characters all appear in Richardson's novels and result from his use of the plots of the drama and his dramatic focus upon character. Muir describes the affinities between the "dramatic novel" and the formal drama: "In formal drama the qualities we have found in the dramatic novel exist in their purity. The confinement to one scene; the isolation of the characters; the unfolding development making towards an end; the conflict; the *dénouement;* all are there as they are in *Wuthering Heights* or in *The Return of the Native.* 'The confinement to one scene' may be contested. In a play the scene changes, of course, but the necessities of dramatic production take away, it might be contended, all great significance from the change."[9]

In opposition to the "dramatic novel," Muir describes the "character novel": "The plot of the character novel is expansive. . . . The action . . . begins with a single figure, as in *Roderick Random,* or with a nucleus, as in *Vanity Fair,* and expands towards an ideal circumference, which is an image of society. . . . The novel of character takes its figures, which never change very much, through changing scenes, through the various modes of existence in society."[10] Percy Lubbock in *The Craft of Fiction* defines a type of fiction similar to Muir's "character novel": he describes Thackeray's "panoramic" presentation as creating "broad expanses, stretches of territory, to be surveyed from edge to edge with a sweeping glance; he saw them [his novels] as great general, typical impressions of life, populated by a swarm of people whose manners and adventures crowded into his memory."[11] "Panoramic" is a better name than "character" for this type of novel, since such fiction attempts to create a large, panoramic view of society through the presentation of a multitude of fixed character types which are representative of various elements of society. On the other hand, the works that Muir calls "dramatic" I prefer to call character novels, since their emphasis is on developed characterizations and character relationships. The differences between the two types of novels are clear when presented in the following manner:

Character Novel	*Panoramic Novel*
1. Focus on a few characters and character relationships.	1. Panoramic view of society.
2. Detailed external and internal presentation of characters.	2. External presentation of characters as fixed societal types.
3. Narration presented through point of view of characters.	3. Narration presented through omnipotent point of view of author.
4. Selected actions organized into unified plot.	4. Large group of actions loosely organized into plot.
5. Constant sense of time in relation to development of characters and character relationships.	5. Developing spatial sense of society.

It seems to me that Richardson began the English character novel, the main tradition of English fiction, to which Jane Austen and Henry James were to belong, while Fielding began the English panoramic novel, the tradition to which Dickens and Thackeray were to belong. Future novelists like George Eliot were to synthesize both forms, but the distinction between these two types of novels is a useful one for discussing most English novels since 1740.

The dramatic dimension that differentiates most modern fiction from earlier fiction necessitates, I believe, that we call the general group of novels written since 1740, including character and panoramic works, dramatic novels. Ortega y Gasset, in an essay on the development of modern European fiction, makes the following useful observation:

> Now, an examination of the evolution of the novel from its beginnings to our day reveals that, from being pure narration which but alludes, the novel has advanced to strict presentation. At first, the narrative as such kept the reader amused through the novelty of the subject. He was as delighted to listen to the hero's adventures as we are to hear what happened to a person we love. But soon adventures by themselves lose attraction, and what then pleases is not so much the fortunes of the personages as their self-presence. We enjoy seeing those people before us and being admitted to their world or atmosphere. From being narrative and indirect the novel has become direct and descriptive. The best word would be "presentative." The imperative of the novel is autopsy. No good telling us what a person is, we want to see with our own eyes.[12]

The qualities Ortega considers basic to the modern novel existed first in English fiction in Richardson's works. *Pamela, Clarissa,* and *Sir Charles Grandison* are the first "presentative" novels in English literature, for they allow the reader to see the characters and be "admitted to their world or atmosphere." We are allowed both to look into the major figures as they expose their inner beings in their letters and to see their behavior in the episodes they describe. Richardson developed both the dramatic point of view and the narrative-dramatic scene—every level in his novel is fully presented. The use of point of view varied with future novelists—some dramatized it through first-person narration, others through third-person, and others hardly at all.[13] But always some level in a novel was presented and given a dimension of reality in order to make the work more than primitive storytelling: the novelist dramatized the internal world of character, the external scene, or both. Fiction had finally come to life.

Notes

INTRODUCTION

[1] See Ernest A. Baker, *The History of the English Novel* (London, 1930), III, 137.

[2] *The Rise of the Novel of Manners* (New York, 1911), 137.

[3] Sherburn, "The Restoration and Eighteenth Century," in *A Literary History of England,* ed. Albert C. Baugh (New York, 1949), 952; Foster, *History of the Pre-Romantic Novel in England* (New York, 1949), 137; Downs, *Richardson* (London, 1928), 166; and McKillop, *Samuel Richardson, Printer and Novelist* (Chapel Hill, 1936), 40.

[4] In *Selected Letters of Samuel Richardson,* ed. John Carroll (Oxford, 1964), 85-86, dated 19 April 1748 (hereafter referred to as *Selected Letters*). Two articles on this subject by R. S. Crane are "A Note on Richardson's Relation to French Fiction," *Modern Philology,* XVI (1918-19), 495-99, and "Richardson, Warburton and French Fiction," *Modern Language Review,* XVII (1922), 17-23.

[5] See Helen S. Hughes, "Translations of the *Vie de Marianne* and Their Relation to Contemporary English Fiction," *Modern Philology,* XV (1917), 491-512, and McKillop, *Richardson,* 36 n.

[6] "Romances in general, and Marivaux's amongst others, are wholly improbable." (Unless otherwise stated, citations from *Clarissa; or, The History of a Young Lady* in my text are to the Shakespeare Head Edition [Oxford, 1930]. The present citation is from VIII, 326.) In a footnote Richardson refers to this essay as "A Critique on the History of Clarissa, written in French and published at Amsterdam." He states, "The whole critique is rendered into English in the Gentleman's Magazine of June and August, 1749" (VIII, 327). The only French fiction with which Richardson did admit a familiarity were the romances. He attacks the "Marvellous and . . . unnatural Machinery" of these works in a letter to Stephen Duck and the "French Marvellous" in a letter to George Cheyne (*Selected Letters,* 53, 54).

[7] Throughout this study I shall refer to part I of Richardson's novel as *Pamela,* as it generally is known in literary history, and to its sequel as *Pamela II.*

[8] *The Rise of the Novel* (London, 1957), 176; see also 31 and 177.

[9] Erich Poetzche in *Samuel Richardson Belesenheit* (Kiel, 1907) lists the dramatic quotations and references to plays that appear in Richardson's fiction and correspondence and makes a general comment about the possible influence of the drama on the novels. Helen S. Hughes in "Characterization in *Clarissa Harlowe*," *Journal of English and Germanic Philology,* XIII (1914), 110-23, discusses the dependence of Clarissa and Lovelace on earlier dramatic types, and Levin L. Schücking in "Die Grundlagen des Richardson'schen Romans," *Germanisch-romanische Monatsschrift,* XII (1924), 21-42 and 88-110, links Richardson's characters

with those in the drama of pathos and sentimental drama. General statements have been made about Richardson's dramatic technique, but there has been no detailed discussion: see Walter Raleigh, *The English Novel* (New York, 1894), 142; Wilbur L. Cross, *The Development of the English Novel* (New York, 1899), 36; Brian W. Downs, *Richardson*, 97; Godfrey Frank Singer, *The Epistolary Novel* (Philadelphia, 1933), 62-63; and Walter Allen, *The English Novel* (New York, 1958), 37. The most developed discussion of the influence of the drama on Richardson's fiction appears in McKillop's *Richardson*, 138-54. Professor McKillop's brief discussion is devoted to *Clarissa* and is concerned mostly with the dramatic background of the hero, heroine, and general plot. George Sherburn in "Samuel Richardson's Novels and the Theatre: A Theory Sketched," *Philological Quarterly*, XLI (1962), 325-29, claims that Richardson's "chief indebtedness to the theatre would be plot-focus, character types, and vivid, extensive conversation" (325). Professor Sherburn is able to give only brief attention to this indebtedness in his five pages, but strongly suggests its importance in the development of fiction (329). And Leo Hughes in "Theatrical Convention in Richardson: Observations on a Novelist's Technique," in *Restoration and Eighteenth-Century Literature,* ed. Carroll Camden (Chicago, 1963), 239-50, discusses the influence of the drama and playbook on the novelist's description of gesture and dress.

[10] See Helen S. Hughes, "English Epistolary Fiction Before *Pamela*," in *Manly Anniversary Studies* (Chicago, 1923), 156-69; Singer, *The Epistolary Novel;* and Robert Adams Day, *Told in Letters* (Ann Arbor, 1966).

[11] Christopher Hill, "Clarissa Harlowe and Her Times," *Essays in Criticism*, V (1955), 315-41; Watt, *The Rise of the Novel;* and Allen Wendt, "Clarissa's Coffin," *Philological Quarterly*, XXXIX (1960), 481-95.

[12] "Richardson's *Familiar Letters* and the Domestic Conduct Books," *Smith College Studies in Modern Languages*, XIX (1938), 1-29. See also Schücking, "Die Grundlagen des Richardson'schen Romans."

CHAPTER ONE

[1] From the letter to the Reverend Johannes Stinstra, dated 2 June 1753, *Selected Letters*, 229.

[2] Citations from *The History of Sir Charles Grandison* in my text are to the Shakespeare Head Edition (Oxford, 1931).

[3] *Selected Letters*, 134.

[4] Richardson mentions Mrs. Behn, Mrs. Manley, and Mrs. Haywood in a letter to Mrs. Chapone, dated 6 December 1750, and located in Forster MS XII. (Much of Richardson's correspondence is in the Forster Collection, Victoria and Albert Museum, London.)

[5] For example, in his Preface and Postscript to *Clarissa*.

[6] This work is credited to Richardson by McKillop in "Samuel Richardson's Advice to an Apprentice," *Journal of English and Germanic Philology*, XLII (1943), 40-54. Professor McKillop has one of the few extant copies of *The Apprentice's Vade Mecum*. My comments are based upon the quotations in his article.

Notes

7 Cited from *ibid.,* 50.

8 Allan D. McKillop, "Richardson's Early Writings—Another Pamphlet," *Journal of English and Germanic Philology,* LIII (1954), 72-75.

9 Vol. IV, Letters XI, XII, and XIII. Citations from both parts of *Pamela; or, Virtue Rewarded* in my text are to the Shakespeare Head Edition (Oxford, 1924).

10 VII, 133-34.

11 In *Samuel Richardson Belesenheit* (Kiel, 1907), Erich Poetzsche compiled the quotations in Richardson's works and letters and assumed that the novelist had taken them from those works which he had read. A. Dwight Culler compared the novelist's quotations with those collected in Bysshe's *The Art of English Poetry* (1702) and decided that he took his passages from Bysshe's work, neglecting to acknowledge his source ("Edward Bysshe and the Poet's Handbook," *PMLA,* LXIII [1948], 871 *n*). For this reason Culler claimed that Richardson's quotations do not necessarily signify the works he read.

12 *Clarissa,* VII, 15.

13 Letters CLVIII and CLIX. The complete title is *Letters Written To and For Particular Friends, On the Most Important Occasions. Directing not only the Requisit Style and Forms To be Observed in Writing Familiar Letters; But How to Think and Act Justly and Prudently, In the Common Concerns of Human Life. Containing One Hundred and Seventy-three Letters. None of which were ever before Published.* There is a modern edition of this work, with an introduction by Brian W. Downs, called *Familiar Letters on Important Occasions* (London, 1928).

14 In 1750 he published *Meditations Collected from the Sacred Books; And adapted to the Different Stages of a Deep Distress; gloriously surmounted by Patience, Poetry, and Resignation. Being those mentioned in the History of Clarissa as Drawn up by her for her own Use,* and in 1751 *Letters and Passages Restored from the Original Manuscript of the History of Clarissa. To which is subjoined, A Collection of such of the Moral and Instructive Sentiments, Cautions, Aphorisms, Reflections and Observations contained in the History, as are presumed to be of general Use and Service.* A similar collection of the wisdom from all three novels was published in 1755. See William Merritt Sale, Jr., *Samuel Richardson: A Bibliographical Record of His Literary Career, with Historical Notes* (New Haven, 1936).

15 See William M. Sale, Jr., *Samuel Richardson: Master Printer* (Ithaca, 1950).

16 Dates are for original productions of plays. See *ibid.,* for the dates of Richardson's publications of these works.

17 Biographical information is from Richard Hindry Barker, *Mr. Cibber of Drury Lane* (New York, 1939).

18 Anna Laetitia Barbauld, *The Correspondence of Samuel Richardson* (London, 1804), II, 178-79 (hereafter referred to as *Correspondence*).

19 *An Apology for the Life of Colley Cibber, Written by Himself,* ed. Robert W. Lowe (London, 1889), I, 266.

20 Biographical information is from Dorothy Brewster, *Aaron Hill* (New York, 1913).

21 The extent of Mitchell's collaboration on the work is unknown.

Notes

22 *The Drama of Sensibility* (Boston, 1915), 132.

23 *A History of English Drama, 1660–1900*, Vol. II: *Early Eighteenth Century Drama*, 3d ed. (Cambridge, Eng., 1955), 119.

24 McKillop, *Samuel Richardson, Printer and Novelist* (Chapel Hill, 1936), 300.

25 *Ibid.*, 300-301.

26 *Memoirs of the Life of David Garrick* (London, 1780), 157. Printed in Brewster, *Aaron Hill*, 131 *n.*

27 Volumes XXVI–XLVII.

28 *Selected Letters*, 224.

29 Richardson did not approve of Tate's adaptation of *King Lear.*

30 In *Some Unpublished Correspondence of David Garrick*, ed. G. P. Baker (Boston, 1907), 23. Printed in McKillop's *Richardson*, 160.

31 *Meropé* and *Irene* were produced at Drury Lane in 1749, and *Coriolanus* at Covent Garden in the same year.

32 Dated 12 January 1748, located in Forster MS XIII.

33 Ralph L. Collins in "Moore's *The Foundling*—an Intermediary," *Philological Quarterly*, XVII (1938), 139-43, argues that *Clarissa* is partly responsible for *The Foundling's* story and characterizations.

34 *Correspondence*, IV, 37.

35 *Selected Letters*, 224.

CHAPTER TWO

1 Simon O. Lesser, "Pamela as Cinderella," *College English*, XIV (1952), 13-17, discusses the psychological appeal to the modern reader of *Pamela* as a Cinderella story.

2 *Samuel Richardson, Printer and Novelist* (Chapel Hill, 1936), 42. The remainder of my paragraph refers to pp. 29-32 of McKillop's book.

3 The popularity of this subject matter during the period is evident from the number of plays produced with "virtue" or "innocence" in their titles, even when the work has little to do with either and the author obviously is capitalizing on a dramatic trend to attract the public.

4 See Morris Golden's *Richardson's Characters* (Ann Arbor, 1963) for an attempt at a psychological exploration of Richardson and his characters.

5 Unless otherwise stated, all citations from plays in my text are to the microcard collection *Three Centuries of Drama*, ed. Henry Wells (New York, 1954).

6 *The London Stage, 1660–1800: A Calendar of Plays, Entertainments & Afterpieces*, Vol. I, Pt. 3: *1729–1747*, ed. Arthur H. Scouten (Carbondale, Ill., 1961).

7 For a discussion of class warfare as a major theme in Richardson's first two novels, see William M. Sale, Jr., "From *Pamela* to *Clarissa*," in *The Age of Johnson* (New Haven, 1949), 127-38.

8 See H. J. Habakkuk, "England," in *The European Nobility in the Eighteenth Century*, ed. A. Goodwin (London, 1953), 19, for a discussion of the relation between marriage and social position in eighteenth-century England.

Notes

9 Ernest Bernbaum, *The Drama of Sensibility* (Boston, 1915), 61, and McKillop, *Richardson*, 31, mention the general similarity between *Silvia* and *Pamela*.

10 See Fielding's *Shamela*. McKillop, *Richardson*, 75-85, discusses other satires and criticisms of *Pamela* during this period, and the topic is explored in detail in Bernard Kreissman's *Pamela-Shamela* (Lincoln, Nebr., 1960).

11 It is not certain that the work was performed (see Part 3 of *The London Stage*, I, 145-47). An earlier and shorter version titled *The Welsh Opera* was produced in 1731.

12 Citations from *The Grub-Street Opera* are to *The Complete Works of Henry Fielding, Esq.,* Vol. IX (New York, 1902).

13 Robin and Sweetisa are satirical portraits of Sir Robert Walpole and his mistress Maria Skerrett.

14 From the letter dated 2 June 1753. Richardson further discussed this source in a letter to Hill, *Selected Letters*, 39.

15 Paul Dottin, *Samuel Richardson* (Paris, 1931), 104, 148, and McKillop, *Richardson*, 27-28.

16 In the first edition of *Pamela II* Mr. B. tells the story of a "Love Quarrel"; Professor McKillop suggests that this narration is Richardson's initial conception of *Clarissa* (*Richardson*, 108-20). The novelist in the letter of 2 June 1753 to Stinstra claimed that both *Clarissa* and *Sir Charles Grandison* were wholly "invention."

17 See H. J. Habakkuk, "Marriage Settlements in the Eighteenth Century," *Transactions of the Royal Historical Society*, XXXII (1950), 15-30.

18 The novel is based upon Aphra Behn's brief tale *The Wandering Beauty* (1698). Blackmore's novel can be read in *Four Before Richardson: Selected English Novels, 1720-1727,* ed. W. H. McBurney (Lincoln, Nebr., 1963).

19 See John Harrington Smith, *The Gay Couple in Restoration Comedy* (Cambridge, Mass., 1948), for a study of the gay lady in the drama of the Restoration period.

20 The play may have been written by Hildebrand Horden (Allardyce Nicoll, *A History of English Drama, 1660–1900,* Vol. I: *Restoration Drama, 1660–1700,* 4th ed. [Cambridge, Eng., 1955], 413).

21 Richardson earlier had treated such a subject in epistle CXXXIII of *Letters Written on the Most Important Occasions.*

22 See Christopher Hill, "Clarissa Harlowe and Her Times," *Essays in Criticism*, V (1955), 329; Habakkuk, "Marriage Settlements in the Eighteenth Century," 17-20; and Ian Watt, *The Rise of the Novel* (London, 1957), 140-43.

23 See Dorothy Van Ghent, *The English Novel: Form and Function* (New York, 1953), 48-52.

24 See Hill, "Clarissa Harlowe and Her Times," 331, and Watt, *The Rise of the Novel,* 155-61.

25 Many of these heroines appear in "she-tragedies," a term used by Rowe in his epiloque to *The Tragedy of Jane Shore* (1714) to describe those plays with suffering heroines as their protagonists. Such dramas were plentiful during the Restoration and early eighteenth century.

26 *Selected Letters,* 79, dated 26 Jan. 1747. The gentleman mentioned

in the letter may be Richardson's early patron (see McKillop, *Richardson,* 120 and 133-34).

27 Samuel Johnson, "The Life of Rowe," in *Lives of the English Poets,* ed. George Birkbeck Hill (Oxford, 1905), II, 67; and H. G. Ward, "Richardson's Character of Lovelace," *Modern Language Review,* VII (1912), 494-98.

28 The novel is printed in *Four Before Richardson.*

29 See also *Spectator* Nos. 203 (by Addison) and 602 (author unknown).

30 *Caelia* was performed for either one or two nights in 1732 (Part 3 of *The London Stage,* I, 254-55). Johnson in his "Advertisement to the Reader" in the publication of the work claimed that the characters of Mother Lupine and her women were ill received by the audience.

31 *The Wife's Relief* (1711) and *The Country Lasses* (*The London Stage, 1660–1800: A Calendar of Plays, Entertainments & Afterpieces,* Pt. 2: *1700–1729,* ed. Emmet L. Avery [Carbondale, Ill., 1960], and Pt. 3: *1729–1747*).

32 Bernbaum, *The Drama of Sensibility,* 165; McKillop, *Richardson,* 144; Allardyce Nicoll, *A History of English Drama, 1660–1900,* Vol. II: *Early Eighteenth Century Drama,* 3d ed. (Cambridge, Eng., 1955), 122.

33 Helen S. Hughes, "Characterization in Clarissa Harlowe," *Journal of English and Germanic Philology,* XIII (1914), attempts to relate *Clarissa* to the heroines of the heroic tragedy and sentimental comedy. See also McKillop, *Richardson,* 147-54.

34 See Allardyce Nicoll's discussion of the heroic tragedy in *Restoration Drama,* 100-31.

35 Printed in McKillop, *Richardson,* 151.

36 *Ibid.,* 212.

37 *The Gay Couple,* 211-15.

38 For an example of the indistinct virtuous heroes who appeared occasionally in fiction, see Mrs. Davys' *The Reform'd Coquet* (1724).

39 See John Loftis, *Steele at Drury Lane* (Berkeley and Los Angeles, 1952), 195-205, for a discussion of *The Conscious Lovers* as an exemplary comedy.

40 *The Gay Couple,* 211-14. The quotations cited here, unless otherwise specified, are taken from Professor Smith's book.

41 Such as Lady Sharlot in Steele's *The Funeral* (1701) and Inanthe in Theophilus Cibber's *The Lovers.*

42 Anna Howe is a gay lady with a humble suitor. Mr. Hickman receives the same abusive treatment as his counterparts in the drama. Richardson first handles such a relationship in epistle LXXXIII of *Letters Written on the Most Important Occasions,* in which a gay lady describes her relationship with her suitor.

43 See Richardson's "Prefatical Hints," in *Clarissa: Preface, Hints of Prefaces, and Postscript,* Augustan Reprint Society (Los Angeles, 1964).

CHAPTER THREE

1 See Ernest Bernbaum, *The Drama of Sensibility* (Boston, 1915), 1-10, for a related discussion of sentimental drama.

Notes

2 See F. W. Bateson, *English Comic Drama, 1700–1750* (Oxford, 1929), 12-13, for a related discussion of early eighteenth-century drama.

3 "Sentimental" at this time meant a refined and elevated use of the emotions, though sentimental literature was not necessarily refined or elevated; it was later that the word meant an indulgence in superficial emotion.

4 For example, James R. Foster in his *History of the Pre-Romantic Novel in England* (New York, 1949). Ian Watt in *The Rise of the Novel* (London, 1957) also ignores the relationship of Richardson's novels to sentimental drama.

5 Arthur Sherbo in *English Sentimental Drama* (East Lansing, 1957) discusses the difficulty in deciding if an eighteenth-century play is a sentimental drama. See John Loftis, *Comedy and Society from Congreve to Fielding* (Stanford, 1959), 127-28, for an argument against the generic use of the term "sentimental comedy."

6 See Joseph Wood Krutch, *Comedy and Conscience After the Restoration,* 2d ed. (New York, 1949).

7 *The Drama of Sensibility,* 10.

8 *Ibid.*

9 Lovelace desires a wife who would be a *"Lady Easy* to all [his] pleasures" (IV, 264).

10 The play appeared as a one-act drama in 1721 and was expanded into two acts and produced in 1722. A printed version of five acts was published in 1726 (see Allardyce Nicoll, *A History of English Drama, 1660-1900,* Vol. II: *Early Eighteenth Century Drama,* 3d ed. [Cambridge, Eng., 1955], 119, 336). My references are to the two-act version.

11 *The Drama of Sensibility,* 10.

12 See Loftis, *Comedy and Society,* for a discussion of the new attitude toward the merchant class in early eighteenth-century comedy.

13 *Selected Letters,* 106.

14 Bernbaum, *The Drama of Sensibility,* 2.

15 Compare Courtine and Sylvia in Otway's *The Souldier's Fortune* (1680) with Inanthe and Eustace in Theophilus Cibber's *The Lover.* See John Harrington Smith, *The Gay Couple in Restoration Comedy* (Cambridge, Mass., 1948).

16 E.g., Sir John in Lillo's *Silvia.*

17 Compare Sir Sampson Legend in Congreve's *Love for Love* with Sir John Bevil in Steele's *The Conscious Lovers.* See Elizabeth Mignon, *Crabbed Age and Youth* (Durham, 1947), 181.

18 Compare Jeremy in *Love for Love* with Trusty in Steele's *The Funeral.*

19 Compare Worthy in Vanbrugh's *The Relapse* (1696) with Sir Friendly Moral in Cibber's *The Careless Husband.*

20 See Bateson, *English Comic Drama,* 12-13.

21 In *Characteristics,* 2d ed. (London, 1714), II, 99. Two interesting discussions of the background of Shaftesbury's writings are R. S. Crane's "Suggestions Towards a Genealogy of 'The Man of Feeling,'" *ELH,* I (1934), 205-30, and Ernest Tuveson's "The Importance of Shaftesbury," *ELH,* XX (1953), 267-99. See also Louis I. Bredvold, *The Natural History of Sensibility* (Detroit, 1962).

Notes

[22] In *Tracts and Pamphlets by Richard Steele,* ed. Rae Blanchard (Baltimore, 1944), 54-55.

[23] From a transcript of a letter written by "Philopamela," dated 21 or 22 March 1742, in Forster MS XVI.

[24] See John W. Draper, "The Theory of the Comic in Eighteenth-Century England," *Journal of English and Germanic Philology,* XXXVIII (1938), 220-21, for a relevant interpretation of comic portrayals in eighteenth-century drama.

[25] Jonson's theory of humours was echoed in such critical writings as Farquhar's *Discourse Upon Comedy* (1702) and Gildon's *The Complete Art of Poetry* (1718); his plays frequently were produced throughout the Restoration and eighteenth century (see Robert Gale Noyes, *Ben Jonson on the English Stage, 1660–1776* [Cambridge, Mass., 1935]). For a discussion of those works directly influenced by the plays of Jonson see Allardyce Nicoll, *A History of English Drama, 1660–1900,* Vol. I: *Restoration Drama, 1660–1700,* 4th ed. (Cambridge, Eng., 1955), 201-18, and Vol. II: *Early Eighteenth Century Drama,* 174-79.

[26] J. E. Austen-Leigh, *Memoir of Jane Austen,* ed. R. W. Chapman (Oxford, 1926), 89.

[27] McKillop, *Samuel Richardson: Printer and Novelist* (Chapel Hill, 1936), 213, makes a relevant point: "It is the gentility of *Grandison* rather than the crude portraiture of *Pamela* or the tragedy of *Clarissa,* that set the tone for the feminine novel of the second half of the century, and established the tradition on which Jane Austen triumphed. *Grandison* showed the way to the substitution of social embarrassment for tragic conflict, to a light transcription of manners, and to a 'delicacy' which was sometimes silly but at its best penetrating and subtle."

CHAPTER FOUR

[1] Samuel Richardson, "Prefatical Hints," in *Clarissa: Preface, Hints of Prefaces, and Postscript,* Augustan Reprint Society (Los Angeles, 1964), 4.

[2] Richardson here is adapting a passage from one of Edward Young's letters (*Correspondence,* II, 5).

[3] *Selected Letters,* 99, dated 7 Nov. 1748.

[4] *Selected Letters,* 104-105.

[5] For a discussion of neoclassic tragic criticism see Clarence C. Greene, *The Neo-classic Theory of Tragedy in England During the Eighteenth Century* (Cambridge, Mass., 1934).

[6] "Preface Containing the Grounds of Criticism in Tragedy," in *Essays of John Dryden,* ed. W. P. Ker (Oxford, 1900), I, 209-10.

[7] *The Critical Works of John Dennis,* ed. Edward Niles Hooker (Baltimore, 1939), I, 35.

[8] *The Complete Art of Poetry* (London, 1718), I, 189.

[9] From Thomson's *Tancred and Sigismunda* (1745).

[10] *Lectures on Rhetoric and Belles Lettres* (Philadelphia, 1844), 520.

[11] *Selected Letters,* 41.

[12] *Ibid.,* 99.

Notes

13 To Lady Bradshaigh, *Selected Letters,* 104.

14 *Ibid.,* 108.

15 *Ibid.,* 105.

16 Postscript to *Clarissa,* VIII, 308.

17 *Ibid.,* 314-15.

18 "Prefatical Hints," 7. This statement appears in a section probably written by the Reverend Mr. Skelton.

19 *Poetics,* trans. S. H. Butcher, in *The Great Critics,* ed. James Harry Smith and Edd Winfield Parks (New York, 1939), 40-41.

20 Hooker, *Works of John Dennis,* I, 19.

21 "An Essay on the Art, Rise, and Progress of the Stage in Greece, Rome, and England," in *The Works of Mr. William Shakespeare,* ed. George Sewell (London, 1728), I, 34. This essay was published originally by Gildon in his addition of a seventh volume to Rowe's edition of Shakespeare.

22 *Remarks Upon Cato, a Tragedy* (1713), in Hooker, *Works of John Dennis,* II, 49-50.

23 It is also of interest that Richardson, reacting to the insensitive readings of his public, made changes and additions in the second and third editions to emphasize certain moral points and to strengthen Lovelace's evil qualities and Clarissa's delicacy; see M. Kinkead-Weekes, "*Clarissa* Restored," *Review of English Studies,* X (1959), 156-71.

24 In *Selected Letters,* 73, dated 29 Oct. 1746.

25 Samuel Crompton, "Richardson's 'Clarissa' Annotated," *Notes and Queries,* VIII (1877), 102.

26 In *Selected Letters,* 201, dated 2 March 1752.

27 "Prefatical Hints," 9-11.

28 "I think, that, with all his preponderating faults, I like him better than I ever thought I should like him; and, those faults considered, better perhaps than I *ought* to like him" (I, 298).

29 See Hooker's "Explanatory Notes" to his edition of *Works of John Dennis,* II, 453.

30 Preface to *Troilus and Cressida,* in Ker, *Essays of John Dryden,* I, 214.

31 Rymer, *A Short View of Tragedy* (1693), in *The Critical Works of Thomas Rymer,* ed. A. Zimansky (New Haven, 1956), 156; Dennis, *Remarks Upon Cato, A Tragedy,* in Hooker, *Works of John Dennis,* II, 53.

32 Preface, I, xii.

33 *Poetics,* 37.

34 *The Tragedies of the Last Age Consider'd* (1678), in Zimansky, *Works of Thomas Rymer,* 26.

35 *Spectator* 40 (April 16, 1711), I (London, 1726), 152.

36 *Some Remarks on the Tragedy of Hamlet,* Augustan Reprint Society (Los Angeles, 1947), 59.

37 In *Spectator* 40.

38 In the Preface to the first edition (I, vi) Richardson says that he had been advised by friends not to prune the work and reduce it to "Dramatic Unity"; but he seems here to be referring not to plot, but to the "Reflections and Observations" and the abundant details of events and characters objected to by some readers.

39 Richardson originally published the work as seven volumes.

Notes

40 *Poetics,* 33.

41 *Development of the English Novel* (New York, 1899), 37.

42 Though unspecified, the duration of *Pamela,* because of the novel's dramatic plot, is less than a year; *Pamela II,* however, covers a period of years. The duration of *Sir Charles Grandison* is approximately fifteen months.

43 Congreve in his Preface to *Incognita* (1692) claims that his work maintains a unity and development of plot found only in the drama, and that the action all takes place within three days. In these respects his novel was unusual.

44 In *The Tragedies of the Last Age Consider'd.* See Hooker's "Explanatory Notes" in his edition of *Works of John Dennis,* II, 436, for a brief discussion of the concept of poetic justice in English literary criticism before Rymer.

45 *Spectator* 40, I, 150.

46 *To the Spectator, Upon his Paper on the 16th of April* (1712), in Hooker, *Works of John Dennis,* II, 19.

47 *The Usefulness of the Stage* (1698), in Hooker, *Works of John Dennis,* I, 183.

48 Later in the century Hugh Blair articulated the attitude of the sentimental critic toward poetic justice. Poetic justice, he claimed, has "been long exploded from tragedy"; the good are allowed to suffer as long as their suffering makes "virtue appear amiable and venerable" and "shall render their condition, on the whole, preferable to that of bad men" (*Lectures,* 520).

49 VIII, 312.

50 In Forster MS XV, dated 5 Dec. 1748.

51 II, 283.

52 *Spectator* 44 (April 20, 1711), I (London, 1726), 167-68, and *The Complete Art of Poetry,* I, 242.

53 Norman Rabkin in "*Clarissa:* A Study in the Nature of Convention," *ELH,* XXIII (1956), 204-17, suggests that Lovelace represents "the 'natural man' in whom recognition of the necessary order of society is virtually absent"; and Clarissa represents "the individual in whom social convention has become embodied to the point that she lives without regard to the just claims of animal nature" (205). Morris Golden, *Richardson's Characters* (Ann Arbor, 1963), sees the struggle between the two as a struggle for dominance. Sounder, I believe, than both of these interpretations is the one by Allen Wendt based on the moral tensions of the period: in "Clarissa's Coffin," *Philological Quarterly,* XXXIX (1960), Professor Wendt sees Lovelace as representing "the appeal of the flesh, which Clarissa must deny," and Clarissa "the appeal of the spirit, which challenges his fleshly kingdom" (485).

54 Clifford Leech, *Shakespeare's Tragedies and Other Studies in Seventeenth Century Drama* (London, 1950), 15.

55 Max Scheler, "On the Tragic," trans. Bernard Stambler, *Cross Currents,* IV (1954), 185.

56 F. L. Lucas, *Tragedy in Relation to Aristotle's Poetics* (London, 1949), 91-94.

134

Notes

CHAPTER FIVE

[1] All citations from *Moll Flanders* in this chapter are taken from the Shakespeare Head Edition (Oxford, 1927). Sheldon Sacks attempts to discuss the differences between the novels of Defoe and Richardson in *Fiction and the Shape of Belief* (Berkeley and Los Angeles, 1964), 267-70.

[2] Eliza Haywood, *Love in Excess; or, The Fatal Enquiry,* in *Secret Histories, Novels, and Poems in Four Volumes Written by Mrs. Eliza Haywood,* 4th ed. (London, 1742), I, 35.

[3] Richardson's "Prefatical Hints," in *Clarissa: Preface, Hints of Prefaces, and Postscript,* Augustan Reprint Society (Los Angeles, 1964), 8.

[4] For a relevant discussion of the vividness of Richardson's episodes see George Sherburn, " 'Writing to the Moment': One Aspect," in *Restoration and Eighteenth-Century Literature,* ed. Carroll Camden (Chicago, 1963), 201-209.

[5] Leo Hughes, "Theatrical Convention in Richardson: Observations on a Novelist's Technique," in *Restoration and Eighteenth-Century Literature,* 247-49, suggests that Richardson may have been influenced in his description of gesture and dress by illustrations in playbooks and Aaron Hill's *Art of Acting*.

[6] See above, pp. 110-11.

[7] Forster MS XV.

[8] *The Structure of the Novel* (London, 1928), 59-60.

[9] *Ibid.,* 147.

[10] *Ibid.,* 59-60.

[11] *The Craft of Fiction* (New York, 1960), 93.

[12] In *The Dehumanization of Art and Other Writings on Art and Culture* (New York, 1956), 57.

[13] Two standard works on the novel which discuss at length point of view are Percy Lubbock's *The Craft of Fiction* and Wayne C. Booth's *The Rhetoric of Fiction* (Chicago, 1961).

Index

Index

Index

Haywood, Eliza: *The Fatal Secret,* 29-30; little realistic characterization, 95-96; *Love in Excess,* 99-100; mentioned by Richardson, 126

Head, Richard, 1

Heroic tragedy, 45-48, 130

Hewitt, John, 36

Hill, Aaron: *Alzira,* 12, 14, 89; *The Art of Acting,* 14, 135; *Athelwold,* 13, 92; *Elfrid,* 13; *The Fatal Extravagance,* 13-14, 59-60, 61; friends with Richardson, 13-14; *Meropé,* 15, 128; *The Prompter,* 14; theatrical career of, 13-14, 16; translated Voltaire's plays, 14; mentioned, 26, 36, 74, 81

Hill, Christopher, 5

Hoadly, Benjamin, 50

Homer, 7

Hopkins, Charles, 30-31, 33

Horace, 75

Horden, Hildebrand, 129

Hornbeak, Katherine, 5

Hughes, John, 18

Humanitarianism in the eighteenth century, 61-62

Humor character in the drama, 54-55, 69-71

Hutcheson, Francis, 62

Italian opera, 9

James, Henry, 6, 121, 123

Johnson, Charles: *Caelia,* 35-36, 37, 40-45, 60, 61, 130; *The Country Lasses,* 21-23, 27, 28, 59

Johnson, Samuel: attack on unities of time and place, 87; introduced Richardson to Baretti, 48; *Irene,* 15, 89, 128; on Lovelace and Lothario, 38; read by Richardson, 7

Jonson, Ben, 69-70, 132

Joyce, James, 6, 121

Kelly, Hugh, 71

Kirkman, Francis, 1

Leanerd, John, 19-21, 23, 27, 28

Lee, Nathaniel, 12, 46, 74

Leech, Clifford, 93

Lesser, Simon O., 128

Lillo, George: *The Fatal Curiosity,* 61, 92; *The London Merchant,* 8-9, 60, 61, 67, 80, 92; *Marina,* 35-36; *Silvia,* 23-25, 27, 28, 59

Locke, John, 8

Lubbock, Percy, 122-23

Lucas, F. L., 94

Lucrece, 33

Lyttelton, Lord George, 15

McKillop, Alan Dugald, 2, 18, 26, 40, 48, 125-32 *passim*

Man of sense in the drama, 49-51

Manley, Mary de la Revière, 126

Index

Sexual morality in the drama, 19, 128

Shaftesbury. *See* Cooper, Anthony Ashley

Shakespeare, William: *Hamlet*, 48, 86-87; impending doom in his tragedies, 92; *King Lear*, 15, 74; *Measure for Measure*, 10; *Othello*, 14, 85, 94; *Pericles, Prince of Tyre*, 35; preferred to ancient dramatists by Richardson, 7; *Romeo and Juliet*, 75; tension before acts of violence in his tragedies, 92; *Troilus and Cressida*, 9-10; mentioned, 13

Sherburn, George, 2, 126

She-tragedy, 33-34, 47, 79, 80, 129

Skelton, Philip, 133

Smith, Alexander, 18

Smith, John Harrington, 49, 50-51

Smollett, Tobias, 2, 5, 122

Some Remarks on the Tragedy of Hamlet, 86-87

Sophocles, 7, 94

Southerne, Thomas, 36, 37-38, 87

Spectator, 62, 81, 90-91. *See also* Addison, Joseph; Steele, Sir Richard

Spence, Joseph, 81, 103

Spenser, Edmund, 7

Steele, Sir Richard: *The Christian Hero*, 62; *The Conscious Lovers*, 49-50, 54, 59, 71; *Spectator*, 29, 39-40; *The Tender Husband*, 9

Sterne, Laurence, 120-21

Stinstra, Johannes, 26

Sturmy, John, 31-32, 33

Tatler, 62

Taylor, Jeremy, 8

Terence, 7

Thackeray, William Makepeace, 121, 122-23

Thomson, James: *Coriolanus*, 15; influenced by Shaftesbury, 62; *Tancred and Sigismunda*, 76, 79, 80

Tillotson, John, 8

Trotter, Catherine, 52

Vanbrugh, Sir John, 54

Virgil, 7

Voltaire, François de, 12, 14

Warburton, William, 3

Ward, H. G., 38

Watt, Ian, 4, 5

Wendt, Allen, 5, 134

Woolf, Virginia, 121

Wycherley, William, 49

Young, Edward: *The Brothers*, 12, 14-15; *Conjectures on Original Composition*, 14; friendship with Richardson, 14-15; quoted by Richardson, 74, 132; *The Revenge*, 14, 15, 79, 85

Yorkshire Tragedy, A, 13

Date Due